THE
ROTTWEILER

Richard F. Stratton

Dedication

To Carlene and Kent Freeman

Front cover photo by Isabelle Francais. **Back cover photo** of Champion Graudstark's Rhapsody courtesy of Rhapsody's owner, Virginia Koerber. Photos on Pages 112, 113, 150, 173, and 175 courtesy of Kent Freeman.

Title page Pomac's Lexa P. Van Lare already showing good type at fifteen months. Owned by Greg and Lori Benkiser.

Distributed in the UNITED STATES by T.F.H. Publications, Inc., 211 West Sylvania Avenue, Neptune City, NJ 07753; in CANADA by H & L Pet Supplies Inc., 27 Kingston Crescent, Kitchener, Ontario N2B 2T6; Rolf C. Hagen Ltd., 3225 Sartelon Street, Montreal 382 Quebec; in ENGLAND by T.F.H. Publications Limited, 4 Kier Park, Ascot, Berkshire SL5 7DS; in AUSTRALIA AND THE SOUTH PACIFIC by T.F.H. (Australia) Pty. Ltd., Box 149, Brookvale 2100 N.S.W., Australia; in NEW ZEALAND by Ross Haines & Son, Ltd., 18 Monmouth Street, Grey Lynn, Auckland 2 New Zealand; in SINGAPORE AND MALAYSIA by MPH Distributors (S) Pte., Ltd., 601 Sims Drive, # 03/07/21, Singapore 1438; in the PHILIPPINES by Bio-Research, 5 Lippay Street, San Lorenzo Village, Makati Rizal; in SOUTH AFRICA by Multipet Pty. Ltd., 30 Turners Avenue, Durban 4001. Published by T.F.H. Publications Inc. Manufactured in the United States of America by T.F.H. Publications, Inc.

Contents

Acknowledgements

I would like to formally thank Larry Katz, dog trainer par excellence, for sharing with me his ideas on training. What appears in this book, however, is an amalgamation of my ideas on training together with those of many other trainers, including those of Mr. Katz. For that reason, Larry should not be held accountable for anything that appears herein, as some of the ideas are not his, and those that are indeed his may have been presented inadequately.

Another trainer of long experience and one of the few people whom I would classify as a true expert on dogs is Gail Ross. As always, she has been helpful with this book, as she has with others in the past.

Finally, I would like to thank the Rottweiler devotees who sent in pictures for this book on rather short notice. I am in particular indebted to Vivian Peters, who not only supplied a plethora of photographs, but who provided advice on what should appear in the book too. If the Rottweiler breed is supported by enough people with the dedication and integrity of Mrs. Peters, there need be no fear for its future—even with the heady popularity that it is now experiencing.

Ch. Pomac's Yoda of Dagobah, bred, owned, and handled by Patrick and Olga McDonald, exemplifies the strength and awareness that are so characteristic of this noble breed. It is the formidable Rottweiler, some sources believe, that marched alongside Roman legions nearly two thousand years ago when they conquered the town of Rottweil in what is now southern Germany. The original German breed standard describes the Rottweiler as a strongly-built, active dog, one that is intelligent, courageous, dignified, naturally obedient, and easily trained to work. Anyone desiring a loyal protection dog *and* an affectionate household companion should consider purchasing one of these splendid dogs!

6

Chapter 1

The Guardian

It seems to be the fashion these days to pooh-pooh the desirability of the guard dog. An associate of mine, however, tells me that potential burglars often size up an area or neighborhood before they strike, and they make a note of the houses to skip because they happen to contain dogs. Further, my friend, who happens to be a police detective, says that with the advent of more and more dogs (because of more and more burglaries), the burglars become selective and hit the houses in which the dogs contained are of breeds that are not likely to be much of a deterrent. So what if they bark! The neighbors have heard the barking before, and the burglars have planned their activities to coincide with your absence, so what good is a barking dog? According to my friend, the police officer, one of the breeds, if not *the* breed, that is most feared by these vermin is the great and mighty Rottweiler.

The unwanted intruders have good reason to fear the Rottweiler, for this is a guard dog without peer. Some of the attributes of a good guard dog are: large size; a fearsome or formidable appearance; a loud or authoritative bark; and last, but most important, if the burglar isn't frightened away, then our guard dog must be willing to use force to stop him. Obviously, the Rottweiler is a large dog but not a "paper giant" as are so many of the giant breeds. His appearance is not unpleasant, but it has a lion-like formidability to it. As for his bark, believe me, it has considerable authority! Now, most Rottweilers, as is the case with most dogs, will need encouragment, at least, and possibly professional training, to ensure that they will actually attack a human intruder. We will cover all this later; but, obviously, there is an important balance to be found here. A dog that attacks all strangers without regard to circumstances would be undesirable (to put it in the mildest of terms). Still, in this day and age, with ever-increasing crime, a dog that will actually protect the home against intruders, attacking them if necessary, is certainly a valuable asset. We will touch on the training aspect of things a little later; however, it is sufficient to say that if called upon to be a "manstopper," there is none better than the Rottweiler.

HISTORY AND DEVELOPMENT OF THE BREED

The Rottweiler owes its great strength to his heritage as a draft dog, and he owes his name to the town of Rottweil, which is on the Neckar River in South Germany. According to some sources, the Rottweiler was brought there by the Roman armies when they conquered the area nearly 2000 years ago. As the story goes, the Romans used the dogs as war dogs, stock dogs (both as drivers and to guard the stock), as beasts of burden, and as camp guards. Truthfully, it is difficult to say that those dogs were Rottweilers, but the art of the time depicts dogs that looked very much like Rottweilers engaged in those very activities. Since so little was written about dogs in early times, we have to rely upon art work primarily for our "window to the past," at least when our subject of study is a dog breed. In this context, then, perhaps the safest statement that can be made is that a strain of fierce and powerful dogs was used for war, as guards, and for hunting large game, such as boar and lion, and that the Rottweiler seems to be one of the descendants of this strain. No wonder this breed is such a highly-praised guard dog.

Perhaps because of the pressing need for protection dogs, the Rottweiler is currently undergoing a tremendous popularity surge. True devotees of the breed are not altogether happy about this state of affairs. Certainly Rottweiler pups bring high prices; however, that is the root of the problem of popularity. True breed adherents and breeders are concerned about maintaining the integrity of the breed. They would never think of breeding to an animal of unsound body or unstable temperament. Those who see in the situation a chance to make a quick killing, though, don't worry about such things. Eventually, nearly every breed that has experienced the rapid surge in popularity that the Rottweiler is currently undergoing has paid the price by a deterioration in the breed . . . thanks to these get-rich-quick schemes. Fortunately, the Rottweiler has adherents aplenty who are devoted to maintaining its quality.

The popularity of the breed today is in sharp contrast to what it was less than a score of years ago when "Rott" fanciers considered, with puzzlement, the amazing popularity of the Doberman Pinscher. You see, the Rottweiler was generally considered to be an important ancestor in the formation of the Doberman breed; and to Rott people, their breed was a "bigger, better Doberman," and yet, it was not experiencing the popularity of its "child"! Of course the Doberman was introduced earlier (about 1910) in the United States. According to legend, the Rottweiler nearly became extinct in 1900. In fact, it was said that in 1905 there was only one Rottweiler bitch in Rottweil. Luckily, however, there were other animals in Germany of the same breed, even if they were few and widely scattered. A small but dedicated group undertook to save the breed, and its success in military and police work piqued the public interest to the extent that the breed was assured a place in German affection. The breed was recognized by the American Kennel Club on April 9, 1935. Although it maintained a solid foothold, it did not become tremendously popular until recent times. Dogs of the breed were used as "demon dogs" in the film *The Omen*, and this seemed to presage the tremendous burst in popularity.

In spite of the fact that the Rottweiler breed had already proven itself an excellent guard dog candidate, the scenes of the breed as a supernatural beast in a rather outlandish movie somehow struck a responsive chord in a number of people. For the dogs shown not only projected a malevolent menace, but they radiated intelligence and were depicted in scenes that demonstrated marvellous agility for such big dogs. I can picture many a couple whose home had recently been burglarized, thinking that it might be worthwhile to look into the breed—whatever it was! In any case, it made the public aware of the breed so that when they saw individuals in public or pictured in books or magazines, they paid attention to what was said about them; and that, undoubtedly, heightened their interest.

IMPRESSIVE CREDENTIALS

Although the breed's agility, strength, size, and intelligence are all quite remarkable, it was another trait that first impressed me. Let me tell you about it.

First, to set the scene, the dogs that I had become accustomed to were dogs such as hounds, very highly-bred animals with marvellous telescopic noses. Not much training was needed with these guys. They were simply taken on hunts from the time they were young dogs, and, eventually, they took to trailing the correct game themselves and to giving voice on the trail. The dogs were bred according to how good a nose they had, the quality of their voice on the trail, and their perseverance at staying at the foot of the tree (once they had treed their prey) until the hunters arrived. Now here were fabulous animals with unique talents, and they were mannerly and tractable, too—especially for kennel dogs. However, and this is the point, once they hit a trail, no command could call them back. The urge to follow the trail is just too strong, and it overrides any human commands irrespective of the individual dog's tractability.

Now in Central Florida, there was a kennel of hunting dogs (hounds mostly) owned by a friend of mine. He had taken up training dogs as an avocation, and he had quite an assortment of dog breeds. He had Redbone Hounds to break to 'coon trails, Leopard Curs (a type of short-eared scent hound), two Airedales, four Pit Bull Terriers, a German Shepherd Dog, and, most impressive of all, a large Rottweiler that was his own personal guard dog for his house and its surrounding compound. A number of dog people, myself included, had watched Jim, the kennel owner, work a number of dogs with an agitator (a man pretending to be the "bad guy" and protected with padding). The Shepherds and Airedales did fairly well. The Pit Bulls, in spite of their reputation as fierce "people-eaters" were actually hard to attack-train, and while the ones that did attack looked most impressive, the knowledgeable dog people among us knew that it was just a game with them. Even so, it was difficult to get them to abort the attack.

After working all the other dogs on the agitator, Jim decided to bring out "Jack," his Rottweiler, for a little refresher course. He had the agitator hide several hundred yards from us. Then Jim went and got Jack and brought him out from the house, which was about fifty yards from the pick-up truck near which several of us were standing. We were the first people Jack saw, and he bolted straight for us. The huge dog covered the ground so quickly, it seemed as though he was nearly upon us before we realized what was happening. We could see blood in his eye, and it looked for all the world as though he were breathing fire! Being seasoned dog people, we knew that our only hope was to remain frozen and not to move at all. That wasn't hard to do, as most of us were scared stiff anyway!

Yet, unaccountably, one of us (who shall remain nameless!) broke and bolted for the truck. The juggernaut bearing down upon us veered off to intercept the guy headed for the truck. By this time Jim had found his voice and called, "Jack! Drop!" Jack dropped as though he had been shot, and Jim came up and put the lead on him. The entire time the dog eyed us reproachfully as prey that had been denied him. And that was what impressed me, for that dog wanted us almost as much as hounds want a raccoon, and yet it was possible by mere voice command to abort the attack. I might have been less impressed, perhaps, if this had been a guard or attack dog in constant training, but that wasn't the case. Jack was Jim's watch dog. He spent some time in the kennel, but most of his time was spent in the house with the family. What is more, Jack had never yet bitten anyone. But he most assuredly would have that day if it had not been for his training (for which a number of us were quite grateful!).

Of course if it had not been for Jack's protection training, he might not have started an attack run against us. Perhaps not, but Rottweilers do have a certain amount of natural guard-dog aptitude. In any case, an important point is that if you are going to have a large and powerful protection-trained dog like a Rottweiler, you must be sure you complete his training: you must establish control before you teach the aggression. To do otherwise is like building a racing car without brakes. Another point is that the Rottweiler is a working breed, and he has been bred to be tractable. This makes him more of an all 'round dog and, perhaps, a better pet for most people than the more specialized Redbone Hound or the American Pit Bull Terrier. To be sure, the two breeds mentioned are often shortchanged for their versatility, and I don't want to be guilty of adding to that. In fact, I am a confirmed admirer of both breeds. Nevertheless, the point needs to be made that some people will never be satisfied with anything less than the tractability of a working breed.

THE RIGHT BREED FOR YOU?

The question needs to be asked, "Is the Rottweiler the breed for everybody?" And to that question, we must confess that he certainly is not. Here is a dog that is huge and powerful, capable of doing untold harm to the wrong person if handled improperly. Not that a trainer or an owner needs to be large and powerful, too. Far from it, for a ninety-pound woman, or child for that matter, could control a Rott with complete assurance. We will discuss training later. However, an irresponsible person, or one who doesn't have the time, or one who is unwilling to give the time, should settle for another breed—or perhaps not keep a dog at all.

There is much to recommend the Rottweiler. He is big and, to many people, he is beautiful. He is sure to attract attention wherever you take him. His short hair and glossy smooth coat make for a clean and odorless house pet. His intelligence and tractability make him a useful companion. Further, if you want more than a pet and a guard and want to indulge in some sort of competition with your dog, there are numerous activities from which to choose. One of the most common, and one of the easiest if your dog has good conformation, is to show your dog. You can learn to handle your own dog, and in so doing you get to know other Rott owners. You can just enter him in local shows or, if he has the quality and you have the show "bug" by this time, you can travel the show circuit.

If you are more interested in training, you can train your dog for obedience competitions and enter him in those. They are a component of nearly every AKC conformation show. And if training interests you, you can save money by doing your own protection training.

Another avenue of competition in this general direction are the Schutzhund competitions. These are combination protection/utility training competitions. Something that is relatively new, which should be a natural for the mighty Rottweiler, are the weight-pull competitions. All of these activities will be discussed in more detail later on.

So we find that the Rottweiler is a gifted breed that has much to give. You'll be proud of the attention he attracts when you take him for a walk, and if you become interested in one of the areas of competition discussed, you'll be proud when your dog succeeds, and you'll learn something about yourself and your dog when he doesn't. But the greatest gift the Rottweiler brings is peace of mind. A night out at the opera, the movies, or whatever your choice, need not be accompanied by the fear of someone entering uninvited into your house during your absence. You'll have a good time knowing that your canine centurion is on duty . . . always the guardian.

Within every canine breed, there is a variation in temperament, and the Rottweiler is no exception. This is why you can't be certain that your own personal companion dog will be a natural protector; it makes sense, then, to have him trained. Ready to spring into action when duty calls is Ch. Pomac's Bamboozler, bred by Patrick and Olga McDonald of Pomac's Rottweilers.

14

Chapter 2

Selecting Your Sentinel

Now, the presumption is strong in this book that Rottweiler owners and prospective owners are primarily concerned with having a protection dog of some sort; that is, a guard dog for the house or a personal protection dog or both. Ideally, then, what you want is a dog that scares off unwelcome visitors and even physically deters would-be burglars. (And it is always important to remember that a burglar is a potential threat to life and limb, too.) As already indicated, the Rott is a superb dog for that purpose. But you don't want the dog terrorizing your friends and your welcome visitors, too! It is very important when you have a genuine canine protector that he not bite or frighten the wrong people. Incidentally, even though your Rott is non-threatening and completely well-mannered around friends, he still may frighten them simply because of his imposing appearance. Good manners and basic human compassion dictate that you confine your animal someplace so that your friends will feel more comfortable. Luckily, most Rotts have an intuitive sense about people, but you can't rely on that completely; there should be some training involved. The selection of your puppy will be dictated to some extent by the degree of training you are willing to provide him, conducted either by yourself or a professional trainer.

PUPPY OR ADULT?

To be sure, you don't have to acquire a Rottweiler as a puppy. You can obtain a full-grown, fully-trained Rott, and there are several advantages in this. First, you have an immediate house dog ready to go to work as a personal and property guard. Also, such dogs come guaranteed to perform as represented, so you aren't taking the (relatively small) risk that your pup won't turn out to be a good guard dog—and this after months of training and feeding! The disadvantage of obtaining a grown dog is that it is an expensive proposition. Rottweiler pups aren't cheap anyway, and if a trainer invests in one, then invests food and training in bringing one up, he isn't about to let a good dog go for peanuts. About the only grown dogs which constitute a "bargain" are ones that have serious flaws of some kind. The flaw might be something acceptable to you, however. The trainer, if a reputable one, will be more than honest with you about the dog's shortcomings.

But let's assume that you've decided to get a pup. In my opinion, it is very desirable to be able to view the pups yourself and make your own selection; so for that reason, it is a good idea to buy locally if at all possible. Look in the Yellow Pages of your phone book under "Kennels" or "Dogs" for boarding kennels. Such places nearly always keep a file of local breeders as a service to the public, so you can obtain a list of Rottweiler breeders from them. Basically, you'll have to use your own judgment about which breeder to patronize. I could give you a list of questions to ask a breeder to ascertain just how knowledgeable he or she is about the breed; however, I somehow feel that might be counterproductive for a good relationship with the breeder!

There are no sure signs to look for other than clean quarters for the dogs and that the dogs themselves are healthy and well trained. It could be a mistake to use the size of the kennel as your guide, as some of the best and most conscientious breeders have been those that ran a small operation and made very few breedings, but those that they did make were meticulously planned and without the expense of a stud fee to the country's outstanding dog being a barrier. Even a person who is relatively

Arinov's family portrait. Arinov's Kola (at five months) is pictured with her dam, Ch. Tulakes Echo, C.D., and her sire, Ch. Pomac's Always A Cinch. Owners: Dan and Lisa Calkins.

new to dogs may make an outstanding breeding under the tutelage of a veteran Rottweiler fancier. So, as you can see, it is difficult to give absolute guidelines on selecting a proper breeder. Fortunately, there are guidelines for selecting a puppy.

SHOW DOG OR WORKING DOG?

One of the first things you need to decide is whether it matters to you if your dog is to be a show candidate. Dog shows are fun—especially if your dog wins—but they are essentially beauty contests. They aren't even that really, for some breeds are certainly not beautiful, and it is show points (i.e., the shape of the head, angle of the neck, topline, etc.) that count. Conformation shows do help maintain a uniformity of appearance in a breed; however, even this can change as the style of the day changes, and a different "type" becomes fashionable. But we will discuss the dog show game later on in more detail. For now, you need to know if you want a dog that is descended from show stock.

If you do want show stock, check into the pedigree of the pups. Don't worry about anything other than the first three generations: the parents, grandparents, and great-grandparents. Dogs further back in the pedigree can be safely disregarded, as their influence is slight by the time we get to the fourth generation. So if you want show stock, you want to see solid show champions in those first three generations. At the very least, that is the ideal. Anything less is a compromise. You can make compromises, of course; just make sure that you realize that this is exactly what you are doing and that each compromise diminishes the prospect of your own dog becoming a champion. More on show-quality Rottweilers in the puppy chapter.

If you are not concerned about getting show stock, then your emphasis switches to working ability. One measure of this would be obedience competitions. Since this is an AKC-sponsored activity, the obedience degrees obtained show up on the pedigree just as the show championships do, except that the obedience titles appear after the name. They are CD, CDX, and UD, with UD being the highest, and, therefore, the most desirable. Other working dog indications are ratings in Schutzhund trials and working-dog competitions. In fact, for potential guard dogs, these would be more important possibly than the obedience ratings.

SOME THINGS TO CONSIDER

All right, now let us assume that you have decided on your needs. Perhaps you're only interested in a show dog. Or you may want a show dog *and* a guard dog. On the other hand, you may just want a good working dog or guard dog and you're really not too concerned about show potential. It is this criteria that you use to select your litter according to your needs and desires. There still remains the task of selecting the pup from the litter. Now, naturally, here you are going to allow yourself the luxury of personal preference. You'll simply pick the one you like the best. Unfortunately, this doesn't always turn out to be as easy as it sounds. To our rescue comes the knowledge that has been bequeathed to us by ethologists, that is, by animal behaviorists, or

18

dog psychologists, if that term suits you better. Legitimate dog ethologists are people like John Paul Scott and John L. Fuller. These men have done research that has been widely reported and referred to. Those who have not done the research are often charlatans or quacks and can be safely disregarded even if they have DVM after their name and write a newspaper column!

Scott and Fuller did all kinds of research on dog behavior and genetics and the connections between the two, but what we will be concerned with here are the maturation levels that these two reported. If you are of a scientific bent, you may be interested in reading Scott and Fuller's book *Dog Behavior: The Genetic Basis* which summarizes much of their experimentation with dogs. Anyway, according to Scott and Fuller, there are "critical" periods in a pup's development, meaning if he doesn't receive certain experiences during these periods, he may not become all that he otherwise could be.

The first period of particular interest to us is one that comes at approximately three weeks of age. By a critical period, Scott and Fuller mean a special time in life when a small amount of experience will produce a great effect on later behavior. At three weeks of age, the senses start to function, and much that the pup will retain for life is learned at this stage in terms of his socialization with other dogs and humans.

Another critical period is from approximately four weeks to twelve weeks. It is during this time that the pup will start to explore and learn. A "pecking order" in the litter is thought to be formed during this period, whereby a dominance hierarchy is established. Because of the importance of this period, there is a clear implication that the pup should be taken home at about eight weeks. Socialization with humans is important during this period.

The next critical period is from about twelve weeks to about twenty-one weeks. During this time, the pup can begin simple obedience training.

The final critical period that we will consider is from twenty-one weeks to thirty weeks. During this period, the pup can be taught much more involved, "serious," training. Keeping these critical periods in mind can give us an edge in our training endeavors.

In the actual selection of a pup, it should be kept in mind that it is important to take the youngster home at eight weeks of age, for the research to which we have referred indicates strongly that the pup will never be all that he otherwise could have been in terms of a working dog if he doesn't get human socialization at this time. Most breeders sell their pups at about that age, but some, being throwbacks to an earlier era when pups had to be shipped by rail, still adhere to three months as the age for pups to go to a new home. Conversely, other breeders may sell their animals at an earlier age. (Not everyone is familiar with the studies by Scott and Fuller.) The best thing to do here is put down your deposit, select your pup, and convince the breeder to keep the youngster until he is eight weeks old. The pup needs the socialization of his mother and siblings up until the eight-week age period.

One of the first decisions to make in regard to the actual selection of the individual pup is which sex you prefer. One of the main disadvantages in choosing a female is her heat cycle, or estrus, which normally occurs twice a year. However, this disadvantage is nullified by having her spayed; but, of course, you will have to figure the cost of the operation as a "disadvantage." Generally speaking, most guard-dog trainers prefer males because they are more difficult to "bluff" and are more natural guard dogs. On the other hand, Larry Katz, owner of Centurion Kennels, whom I consider a candidate for the most knowledgeable dog trainer that I've known in my forty years with dogs, tells me that the Rottweiler is one of the few breeds in which the females are good protection dog prospects too. So if you have a particular preference for female dogs, you don't have to rule one out just because you want a guard dog—at least, not if it's a Rottweiler.

A second consideration is the pecking order we were talking about earlier in regard to the critical stages of a dog's learning maturation. It is not clearly understood what establishes a pecking order, for it is not always the biggest pup that is the dominant one, nor is it the smallest pup that is the subordinate one. That is quite often the case—but not always. Apparently, there are other factors, such as genetic predisposition, that help determine pecking order. Also, it should be noted that some dogs may be submissive to other dogs, but they will stand up to humans. Conversely, some dogs can be quite timid or submissive with humans but are a terror to other dogs! Generally speaking, however, the pup that is at the top of the pecking order is the one that has the most self-confidence and will most likely make the best guard-dog candidate. Unfortunately, if he follows true to form, he will also be a little more bull-headed than the other pups in the litter; hence, he may be a trifle more difficult to train, in the sense that he may require more persistent and firmer corrections. After all, he is used to having things *his* way, and he is not about to let that situation be changed easily.

Most trainers would select the dominant pup (i.e., the one at the top of the pecking order) simply because, in theory at least, he is the one that will be the most self-assured and have the most self-sufficiency. He also will stand up to a lot of correction and not become easily cowed. Still, the dominant pup may not be the one for you, as you may want a more tractable dog, one that doesn't need hard correction or special handling. It may be that one of the pups in between the top pup in our pecking order and the bottom one may work out better for you. He'll still be a good protection dog but more amenable to gentle correction.

The pup to avoid is the shy one. It is highly unlikely that it will ever mature into a good protection dog. The pup may be shy because it is at the bottom of the pecking order or the shyness may be genetically related. In fact, the preponderance of evidence suggests the latter; however, the two causes no doubt reinforce each other.

The question is: How do you recognize the dominant pup? Well, there are a series of tests that are designed to do just that. In fact, some of the tests purport to identify the entire litter in regard to rank, utilizing the Greek alphabet. Thus, you have an "alpha" pup, a "beta" pup, a "gamma" pup, a "delta" pup, and so on in descending order depending on how many pups there

Rottie pups seem to love tennis balls! This youngster, Baron Von Haus Hayes, by Ch. Sciroco's Secretariat ex Ivon Vom Lohnert, is owned by Patrick and Olga McDonald.

are in the litter. All of these tests have one thing in common, however; none of them are scientifically proven mainly because that would be very difficult to do. For that reason I won't bother going into them, but they may be something you might want to look into if you're really insistent about being sure that you get an "alpha" pup. (But even then, you won't be absolutely certain!)

So use your judgment and pick the pup you like best, just making sure that he is not shy. Shyness, at least, is a trait that is not difficult to spot. The shy pup is the one that hangs back, perhaps not coming up to you at all. Now, let me just interject here that the shy dog is often intelligent, and many people believe that it is possible to have a relationship with a shy dog that you just don't get with any other kind because they become so wrapped up with their owner, as compared to a stranger whom they want nothing to do with.

However, a shy dog is not likely to make a good protection dog, and he most assuredly will do poorly in the show ring. For that reason, you probably will want a pup that is not shy. If you want to identify the "alpha" pup, even if it is just to avoid get-

22

ting him, he is very likely the one that pushed past all the others to get to you. All the pups in the litter (with the exception of a possible shy one or two) want attention, but he is the one that gets the most of it, practically demanding it.

Apart from making sure your pup is healthy, has the desired elements in his pedigree, and suits your fancy in just about every way, there is one test you may wish to perform with your prospect. Get him off by himself with a tennis ball and see if you can get him to retrieve it for you. For some reason, pups that will learn this readily seem to turn out better as working dogs. Clarence Pfaffenberger, who worked with guide dogs among others, discovered that the trait of retrieving a ball was the single most important test in respect to predicting the ability of some pups to be good guide dogs. This fact becomes all the more interesting when we consider that the guide-dog people had worked out an entire series of tests designed to select future successful guide dogs. Pfaffenberger hypothesized that such pups indicated that they liked to do things for people. Possibly. But, whatever the reason, the test seems to work, as I've talked to trainers who have used it with success as a test for selecting dogs for general all-around working aptitude.

Since the Rottweiler is a large breed, you will want to make sure that the parents of your pups are OFA-certified. In fact, it would be even better to have a pup whose parents *and* grandparents have been so certified. OFA stands for the Orthopedic Foundation for Animals, and they have provided a series of X-ray examinations to confirm an animal is free of hip dysplasia. Certificates are then issued by the OFA to those animals that are HD-free. Hip dysplasia (HD) is a congenital malformation of the hip sockets and/or femur bones that can result in a crippling of the dog in the rear end. It strikes show dogs, and the giant breeds in particular, especially hard. Fortunately, reputable breeders have their breeding stock X-rayed, and they select animals from a long line of tested stock. Most reputable breeders will replace pups that become dysplastic; however, prevention is much more to be preferred, as a pup may be a year old or more before he shows signs of hip dysplasia.

Osso von Rettberg, owned by Mrs. Dorothy C. Lynch. Photo: Louise Van der Meid. The healthy glow of this fine specimen is due, in large measure, to good nutrition.

Chapter 3

Feeding

Providing your dog with a nutritious diet throughout his life will supply him with a natural ability to fight off many diseases and live a long, healthy life. Proper nutrition is no longer a complicated task, as today's commercially available dog foods have been prepared to supply your dog with all of his basic food needs.

WHEN TO FEED

Although one generous meal a day will suffice, the most common feeding pattern among today's dog owners is to give a small meal or just a few dog biscuits in the morning and a big meal in the late afternoon or early evening. This system originated with the use of herding dogs. Since food tended to make the dog sluggish, he was fed after he finished his day's work. Owners of guard dogs, who work primarily at night, reverse the usual pattern and feed the dog his big meal in the morning—which is after work for the dog. This pattern should not be followed for growing puppies, who may need up to four meals a day. Most dogs grow in two years, the equivalent of what it takes humans twenty-five years, so maintain an adequate diet during this high growth period and decrease intake thereafter.

TYPES OF FOOD

Dogs have tolerant digestive systems that are well adapted to handling concentrated foods, such as meat. Their diet must be high in protein and have a sufficient amount of carbohydrates, fats, vitamins, and minerals. Clean, fresh water is an essential requirement and should be available at all times and changed daily.

Today's commercially prepared name-brand foods are the product of years of research into nutrition and are convenient and economical. These products are generally fortified with vitamins and minerals to supplement the natural value of the ingredients, which can suffer a substantial vitamin loss during processing.

There are three main types of prepared foods: dry, semimoist, and canned. The dry food is the most economical and generally requires only the addition of water (or it can be served "as is"). However, dry food may not contain enough fat, so you should add some meat scraps or broth to increase the nutritional value. One disadvantage—from the dog's point of view—is that dry food may be quite tasteless and it often becomes mushy when water is added, thereby sticking to the roof of the dog's mouth. The semimoist cereals or burgers have been judged more palatable, although generally there are more preservatives added to these products than to others. A small percentage of dogs react to these additives by scratching or biting at their skin, in which case the diet should be changed. Canned food is very popular with dogs and can be added to dry foods or cereals or served on its own. While it is the most expensive prepared food, it is not essential that the dog be fed canned food each day. Two or three servings a week should suffice. A diet of strictly canned food encourages the build-up of tartar on the dog's teeth, as there is no texture in the food to abrade the tooth surface. A diet combining several of the food types, aided by an occasional nylon chew bone (Nylabone®), will serve your dog well.

When selecting a particular brand of dog food, read the label for the product's contents and an analysis of its ingredients. The main ingredients are listed in order of content amount. The protein element should be among the first three ingredients. Do not buy a canned food that contains more than 75% water, as you are not getting much product for your money. Compare several brands before making your final selection, and be sure to choose one that is nutritionally complete and balanced as recommended by the National Research Council.

Some meats—canned or fresh—can be irritants to a dog's system. A small number of dogs have been found to be allergic to beef products that contain chemical additives to prevent spoilage. For some dogs, pork is hard to digest, while others experience diarrhea after eating liver. Be alert for signs of distress if you feed these meats to your dog. Older dogs often suffer from kidney problems and a heavy meat diet often overloads their systems with excess protein. Your veterinarian will generally prescribe modifications to the diet of older dogs to avoid health complications.

HOW MUCH IS ENOUGH?

A growing puppy should be plump, but as he grows he loses this "baby fat" and grows into a lean, firm adult. To determine if your dog is properly fed, run your hands over his ribs and hip bones. If these bones are very easily seen or felt, he may be underweight. If the bones are padded and hard to find, he may be overweight.

An overweight dog is the product of too much food and too little exercise. To help a dog regain his proper weight, cut back slightly on the amount of food you give and substitute low-calorie foods, such as raw green beans, low-fat cottage cheese, and cooked vegetables. These foods add bulk but not a lot of calories. Increase his physical activity, slowly at first, and maintain this higher level of exercise to keep off all lost weight and to tone the muscles.

All dogs will benefit from receiving nutritious table scraps with their meals. Most vegetables, cereals, and fruits are good additives, but do not give your dog any sweets or products with sugar, seasoned meats, or vegetables that produce gas (Brussels sprouts, cabbage, or broccoli).

At mealtime, allow the dog an adequate amount of time to

finish his meal (twenty to thirty minutes). If any food remains in the feeding dish after this period, remove and discard it. If this pattern occurs several times, cut back on his rations until the dog finishes his meal in one visit to the dish. Serving more food than his hunger calls for encourages overeating and obesity, which can be life-threatening in dogs. As his activity levels change, you may have to increase or decrease the amount of food you give him to correspond to his needs. In the winter, if your dog spends a considerable amount of time outdoors, you should increase his daily rations by approximately 20% to help him maintain his body heat. Feed him additional fats and foods of high caloric content.

While most dogs will eat the same food every day without complaint, it is advisable to offer a slight variation every now and again. By serving a variety of foods you can avoid potential stomach or bowel troubles that can occur when his intake is forced to change due to your travel plans or to shortages of his usual food. Should you need to change your dog's diet from one main food to another, try to make the changeover as gradual as possible by first adding just a small amount of the new food to his regular meal. Increase the portion of new food daily—watching for signs of digestive distress—until he is accustomed to it.

PROBLEM EATERS

Should your dog be a "picky" eater, there are several methods that may help to stimulate his appetite. Give him only a half ration every once in a while to make him hungrier and more agreeable about eating what is given him. This does not mean that you should starve him, however. Chicken and liver are usually temptations that even a picky eater cannot refuse, as are small amounts of cheese. Do not give these as meals or between-meal snacks, as this may make him even more finicky. Adding a teaspoon of brewer's yeast (for every thirty pounds of body weight) to his meal is said to improve the appetite, but monitor the dog closely after use as this yeast has been associated with stomach bloating in some animals.

If your dog is a good eater and is still underweight, try switching to a different brand of food and supplementing his meals with meat scraps, cooked eggs, and cottage cheese. You may want to have your veterinarian check for the presence of worms or another disorder, should this augmented diet fail to put some weight on the dog. While a healthy dog may skip a meal now and then, if your dog should refuse his food for more than two days, consult your veterinarian.

The "gulper" is the opposite of the picky eater. He is so eager for his food that he takes large mouthfuls and quickly empties his bowl. Such a method of eating often results in a mess, as the dog's stomach cannot handle the sudden onslaught of food and the dog vomits the food back. A gulper is also taking in a lot of air with his food, which could encourage a life-threatening condition called *bloat*. To slow the gulper down, divide his daily rations into several small meals and give them to him at regular intervals. Monitor him. As his eating improves, increase the size of the meals until they are of normal proportion. Another method is to use a very large feeding dish and place a few large, inedible objects (such as nylon bones) in the bowl as obstacles to his eating. Having to maneuver around the objects will slow him down considerably. The gulper will usually grow out of the habit as he matures, as the gulping is often a habit he picked up as a young puppy when he felt it necessary to beat his littermates to the food source. Once he is assured that he will be able to get his fill, even if he dawdles a bit, he should settle into a normal eating pattern.

VITAMINS AND MINERALS

Many nutritionists claim that vitamin and mineral supplements can help pets live longer, healthier lives. While most commercially available foods for dogs have been enriched during preparation to include all the essential nutrients, there are certain situations where dogs may require additional doses of certain elements. One of the clearest cases is when an overweight dog is put on a restricted intake diet. As the amount of food the dog receives is reduced, so is the amount of vitamins and minerals that he is obtaining from his diet. You should consider giving a vitamin supplement to ensure proper nutrition if the dog is to remain on this low-calorie diet for an extended period of time.

Vitamin E has been shown to help improve a poor coat and help clear up minor skin irritations. Vitamin supplementation is commonly used to help bitches whelp faster and easier by replacing the elements that are divided from the mother to the puppies during pregnancy.

Some owners believe that brewer's yeast, which is rich in vitamin B-complex, is a natural flea repellent and a safer choice than chemical pesticides. Adding a little (one teaspoon per thirty pounds of body weight) of the yeast to the dog's food is said to produce a sulfurous taste on the dog's skin that the fleas don't like, so they leave him for a more suitable host. Others believe that frequent scratching or biting at the skin is a sign of vitamin deficiency which can be cleared up by supplementation.

Infirm older dogs have reportedly been aided by receiving daily doses of vitamins C and B-complex. These vitamins are said to help alleviate joint discomfort and allow the dog to move more freely. On a similar note, there is a claim (as yet unconfirmed) that high doses of vitamin C can help stop hip dysplasia, a crippling genetic hip disorder commonly found in the larger breeds. Some breeders believe that supplementing a pregnant bitch's diet with vitamin C will aid in producing puppies that are less prone to hip dysplasia. Others believe that high doses of this vitamin should be given to puppies during their high-growth periods to help prevent the disease and that high doses of vitamin C will keep the disease from progressing in dogs already exhibiting signs of this abnormality. It must be stressed that these claims are still under investigation and currently very controversial.

CHEWING

Throughout the dog's life there is a strong need for him to chew. As a puppy, chewing assists in cutting the puppy teeth and assuring normal jaw development. As he grows, the dog must chew to help rid himself of the baby teeth and make way for the permanent teeth, which appear at four to seven months. This teething process continues for more than a year as the teeth and jaw bones develop.

Without proper chewing diversions, a young dog can be very destructive, often destroying hundreds of dollars worth of household items. Shoes and items made of leather are favorite selections, as well as the more dangerous electric cords, which can cause injury and death.

Even as the dog matures past this critical period of development, the need to chew remains. Chewing on abrasive surfaces is the only way a dog knows to rid his teeth of the irritating tartar or plaque that accumulates at his gum line. Left unchecked, such tartar will erode the enamel of the teeth and eventually destroy the teeth at the roots.

Emotional factors such as loneliness, fear, or boredom bring on bouts of destructive chewing. Left confined or alone for long stretches of time, dogs often find relief in chewing their tensions away.

Since it is inevitable and, in fact, beneficial for dogs to chew, conscientious owners must supply their pets with a nondestructive outlet for these chewing energies. The main point to remember is that the dog must not be allowed to chew an item that is potentially dangerous to him. It must appeal to his chewing instincts, yet be safe and durable. Dogs should never be allowed to chew on an object that can break into sizeable chunks, which when swallowed can pierce the walls of the stomach or intestines. Indigestible items, such as rubber toys or cheap plastic bones, can become lodged in the dog's intestines if swallowed, requiring emergency surgery to remove this blockage before it leads to a painful death.

The chewing of bones can be a useful means of tooth cleaning for the dog, but you should avoid giving your dog bones that splinter— especially those from chicken, turkey, and fish. While most animal bones are flexible when raw, after cooking they become brittle and can cause damage to the dog's mouth and digestive tract. Beef shin or marrow bones, in approximately six-inch lengths, are very sturdy and popular with dogs whose

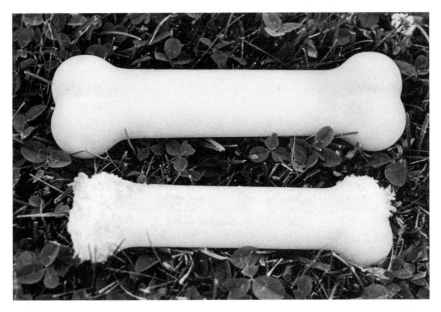

Nylabone® is the perfect pooch pacifier, as it diverts a dogs chewing tendencies and channels his energy into something more constructive. These hard nylon bones, available at pet shops everywhere, are recommended by veterinarians.

Puppies and young dogs need something with resistance to chew on while their teeth and jaws are developing. Nylabones help induce growth of the permanent teeth and assist in getting rid of the puppy teeth.

mouths are large enough to accommodate them. Such bones are, however, highly abrasive. If your dog chews excessively, the use of such bones may cause his teeth to become dangerously worn down in a few years' time, leaving them in a painful, irreparable condition.

Rawhide products are quite popular, but they do not fulfill the dog's chewing requirements very well. Once given to the dog, they quickly become very messy as the rawhide gets wet from mouthing. Most dogs are able to quickly chew them up, making them uneconomical. Additionally, research in the last few years has shown that rawhide pieces can become lodged in a dog's throat and these have been responsible for a number of deaths. The rawhide chunks mix with the saliva in the throat and swell, cutting off the air supply and causing the dog to asphyxiate. Undigested pieces of rawhide have also been associated with cases of severe constipation, as they can cause intestinal blockage.

Nylon bones are generally considered the most economical and safe chew items for dogs. While they are quite sturdy and long-lasting, they are at the same time unabrasive to the surface of the dog's teeth. Hard chewing causes the surface to give off bristle-like shavings that effectively clean the tooth surface and massage the gum line. When swallowed by the dog, these shavings are broken down by the dog's digestive juices and they pass harmlessly through the dog's system. Because of the toughness of the nylon, dogs cannot break off large chunks of the bone, which makes them safe alternatives to animal bones. Nylon is also more sanitary than other material used to make bones, as it does not support the growth of micro-organisms and can be easily cleaned with soap and water.

As a dog requires the use of his teeth throughout his life, owners should routinely inspect the condition of the dog's mouth. While vigorous chewing should keep tartar build-up to a minimum, most dogs will require a professional tooth scraping at least once or twice in their adult life. Be alert to any changes in your dog's eating or chewing behavior for signs of possible distress.

Eleven-week-old Pomac's Lexa P. Van Lare, owned by Greg and Lori Benkiser, relaxes while her feline friend washes its paw. There are a number of provisions that have to be made before you bring home your new Rottweiler companion (setting up a feeding station, providing a dog bed, making an appointment with the veterinarian, to name just a few), but something many pet owners overlook is how they will handle introducing their new pet to those furry critters who are already established family members. In time, each pet will learn to tolerate the other; but in the beginning, it would be wise to separate all parties concerned and bring them together for short intervals under your close supervision.

Chapter 4

General Husbandry

A nutritious diet and adequate exercise are necessary requirements for keeping a dog in good physical condition. The most obvious sign that your dog is not getting enough exercise is excess weight, but there are other indications. If your dog is overactive or restless in the house, he may need more time outside for vigorous activity. Pets with excess energy may show signs of anxiety or become destructive in the house. A dog in good physical condition is better able to withstand disease, remain mentally alert, and live a longer life.

To test your dog's physical trim, feel his muscles in the shoulder and thighs. They should be firm and not soft and flabby. A droopy undercarriage is also evidence that more exercise is needed.

All dogs kept as housepets need to be taken out regularly, at least three times a day to relieve themselves and be exposed to some fresh air. In addition, most dogs will benefit from at least twenty minutes of vigorous exercise. If you live in the city, daily workouts may necessarily be limited to walks and an occasional run in the park. Country dogs, on the other hand, have greater opportunities for exercise. Swimming is an excellent activity that works all the muscles, and most dogs love it. Another favorite exercise—one that is easy on the dog owner—is to have the animal chase and retrieve a ball or stick. This game can be played not only outdoors, but indoors as well, which can be very useful during periods of inclement weather. If you have access to a large amount of open land, try tossing a frisbee for your dog to retrieve. This is an excellent overall exercise and most dogs love the chasing and leaping that are involved. *Warning*: golf balls do not make suitable toys. They are made under great pressure and have been known to explode upon hard contact.

If your dog has a sedentary life and you wish to help him get back in shape, increase his activity level very slowly to avoid overexertion or strained muscles. This is especially important for older dogs. They still need exercise, but in moderate amounts. One extra walk a day will quickly build a dog's stamina.

In times of extreme weather, take precautions when exposing the dog to the elements. In the heat of summer, curtail all vigorous activity during the hottest times of the day and exercise the dog only in the cool of the late evening or early morning. Be sure to have plenty of fresh water available at all times to help prevent heatstroke. In the winter, dogs that are normally confined to the warmth of the house can be very sensitive to great drops in temperature. To avoid a chill and possible illness, supply the dog with a sweater during very cold periods and always be sure to thoroughly dry him once he has come back into the house. This is especially important for older or infirm dogs who can quickly succumb to illness.

When walking the dog at night, a piece of reflective tape on his collar will help make him more visible to motorists.

DOG HOUSES

If your dog is to spend a considerable amount of time outdoors, he will need to have protection from the elements. He will need a place to find shade in the summer and shelter in the winter. If possible, he should be supplied with cover that is well insulated, one that is warm in cold weather and stays cool in the

36

When this crew shows up at the lake, it's hours before their feet touch shore again! Photo courtesy of Patrick and Olga McDonald, Pomac's Rottweilers.

heat of the summer.

For one dog, a dog house would seem the logical choice. It should not be so heavy as to be immovable and it must be placed on ground that drains well. The bottom of the house should never be placed directly on the ground so that it can quickly rot but should be slightly elevated to help keep dampness to a minimum. This can be done by placing two or three bricks under each corner of the house or by building legs that extend six or eight inches from the bottom. The dog house should be painted white, as this helps to repel some of the sun's rays and keep the temperature lowered inside during the summertime.

Whether you build your own dog house or purchase a ready-made version, there are several important features to keep in mind. The house should be constructed of weatherproof materials, with shingles or siding nailed onto the roof to help supply insulation. You should try to draft-proof the house. One way is to nail pieces of carpet or canvas to the door frame; these act as a curtain against the wind. Two pieces that overlap down the center work best to stop the wind from penetrating. A more effective method of preventing drafts is to partition the house into two separate compartments: a large sleeping chamber and an entrance hall. The door should be rather small—yet large enough to allow the dog to enter comfortably—and placed at the extreme left or right along one of the long sides of the dog house. By inserting a wall about half the width of the house to line the entranceway, the inner compartment is kept protected from the elements. A sill two or three inches high at the foot of the doorway also helps reduce drafts and keeps snow out in the winter. Regardless of dog-house style, it is advisable that a section of the roof or one of the sides be hinged for ease in cleaning and changing the bedding.

Bedding is an important part of the dog house. It supplies both warmth and comfort and helps protect your dog from getting sores and callouses on his elbows and hocks. The dog house should be routinely disinfected and the bedding changed frequently, as soiled bedding will attract such annoying pests as fleas, ticks, and lice. In the summer, four to five inches of straw, wood shavings, or shredded newspaper work best. In the winter you can add a blanket or an old mattress pad for more warmth; since these items absorb moisture easily, they must be checked daily for dampness.

PROTECTION FROM THEFT OR STRAYING

As the owner of a purebred dog, you recognize the beauty and quality of your pet. Most likely, he is viewed not only as a pet but as a member of your family. You should be aware that each year thousands of dogs are stolen, often because their owners let the dogs roam or left them unattended. The most common theft pattern occurs when dog owners tie their charges outside of a building or store while they "run a quick errand." Upon returning, their beloved pet is gone. Such a loss could be prevented with a few common sense actions. First and foremost, if you are going someplace where the dog cannot be allowed inside with you, *leave the dog at home.* Second, never allow your dog to run free without direct supervision. Regardless of how well trained

38

he is, he can be lured away. Third, prepare for a potential loss by seeing to it that the dog can be properly identified.

In recent years tattooing has become a very popular method of ensuring that your dog could be identified if he were to become lost or stolen. Tattooing is a relatively painless procedure that can be performed by most veterinarians for a modest fee. If done properly, there is very little risk of infection and the tattooing can be done in several minutes' time.

Tattooing is usually performed on the groin area or inside the ear, although the groin is preferable since there have been reports of dogs having their ears cut off to rid the dog of his identification. Two types of numbers are generally used: the owner's social security number or the dog's AKC registration number. In the case of purebreds, the registration number is most often used to eliminate problems should the dog change owners during his lifetime. Several national registries exist that will record, for an annual fee, the dog's tattoo number and the name, address, and telephone number of his owner. Such registries have led to the safe return of many lost and stolen dogs. Your local kennel club should be able to supply you with the name and address of a registry in your area.

It is best to wait until your puppy reaches at least four months of age before having him tattooed, as you do not want to risk having the tattoo ink smear as the puppy grows and his skin stretches. For owners considering a show career for their dog, there is no reason to forego tattooing. The American Kennel Club has ruled that a tattoo is acceptable in show competition and cannot be penalized.

TRAVELING AND MOTION SICKNESS

One of the greatest pleasures of owning a well-trained dog is being able to enjoy his company wherever you go. If you wish your dog to be a traveling companion, start him off while he is still a puppy. Take him on short trips around town as well as on long drives. Through such exposure, traveling in the car will become routine and great fun.

The first few trips in the car should be short ones, and you

This eleven-month-old bitch, Cassandra vom Hochfeld, has correct conformation but she needs time to mature. Owned by Randall P. and Debora A. Wagner, Cassandra has been obedience trained and temperament tested. Vivian Peters, breeder.

should crate the dog for safety. It is advisable to have another passenger along with the driver to comfort the dog should he become frightened. Be prepared for an emergency clean-up, as young pups often relieve themselves out of fright or vomit in reaction to the unfamiliar motion. Drooling is a sign that the dog is not feeling well, so watch him carefully and let him out of the car at the first hint of sickness. Hopefully this will pass as the dog matures and learns how to relax while riding in the car. If your dog is prone to messes, you may want to line the crate with a towel or some newspapers to aid in the inevitable clean-up. Repetition is the best method for accustoming the dog to the car; do this by gradually lengthening the trips as the dog begins to adjust.

Most dogs take easily to traveling by car, but some are always physically upset by the motion. If this is the case with your dog and he does not outgrow this tendency toward motion sickness, consult your veterinarian about possible remedies.

For trips longer than just around town, there are several steps that may help your dog feel more comfortable during his confinement in the car. To help prevent nausea, never feed your dog a meal before traveling. Wait several hours after he has eaten before leaving on an extended trip. It is recommended that you take the dog for a brisk walk before leaving, both to give him a chance to relieve himself and to tire him a bit. He is more likely to settle in and take a nap while riding if he has been given an opportunity to release some energy before starting the trip. You should give him a drink of water *after* the drive, as the excitement of the trip will make him quite thirsty. If the trip is longer than one hour, plan on stopping halfway to give him a small drink and a chance to relieve himself.

AIR TRAVEL

In recent years traveling in an airplane has become much safer for animals, as stricter rules have been imposed on the airlines to insure the safety of their cargo. You should, however, investigate the safety record of the airlines you are considering, as some companies are more experienced and accommodating than others.

Try to arrange for as short a flight as possible, with a straight-through flight being preferable if at all possible. Be sure the dog's crate, as well as the dog himself, is properly identified. If you are not traveling with the dog, be sure to have a reliable source meeting the dog upon arrival at his new location. Give this person the name of the airline, the number of the flight, and the departure and arrival times. Make sure that this person agrees to contact you as soon as the dog arrives, as dogs have been known to get lost in flight and time is of the essence in locating a misdirected dog crate.

Crates can be purchased from pet shops or they are often available for rent from the airlines. The crate must be sturdy and only large enough to let the dog stand and change positions. If too large, the dog could be easily jostled and possibly injured. On the outside of the crate, plainly write the dog's destination, as well as your name and address. If there are any special instructions (such as possible medical problems), attach these to the outside of the crate where they can be easily read. If it is to be a long flight, you must also include feeding and exercise instructions. A health certificate should be obtained from your veterinarian and included with the dog to prove he has had his rabies and distemper inoculations, as some states will require this before the dog is released.

To make the trip as stress-free as possible, do not feed the dog for four or five hours before the flight. He must be exercised and allowed to relieve himself directly before and after the flight. Include a small amount of dry food in an attached container inside the crate and make sure there is an empty water dish attached to the inside of the crate also. It should be located on or near the door so that it can be filled by the airline personnel with little difficulty. Make the crate familiar to your dog by placing a favorite toy and his usual blanket inside.

If the dog appears overly nervous in his crate, you may wish to give him a mild tranquilizer before the flight. Consult your veterinarian for his advice on travel procedures and sedating animals before a flight.

BOARDING YOUR DOG

Situations occasionally arise when you must be separated from your dog for an extended period of time. If you are planning a vacation or trip in which your dog cannot be included, plan in advance for his care while you are away.

Whatever method you select, put the dog's welfare first. The least traumatic solution would be to leave the dog at home, in his familiar surroundings, and hire a friend or neighbor to care for him. He should not be given free run of the house while unattended, but left confined to a suitable area. The dog will have to be walked and fed several times a day, and, hopefully, the person you select will give him some companionship and attention to keep him from becoming lonely (which can lead to destructiveness). Make sure the person you choose is reliable, and phone him a day or two into your trip to make sure that all is going well. This method is highly stressed for dogs that tend to be

An outdoor kennel should be constructed of sturdy materials and should offer room for your Rottweiler to exercise. Rottweilers allowed outdoors should always be confined to an enclosed area rather than be allowed to roam the neighborhood.

high-strung, aggressive with strangers, or excessive barkers.

If you are planning to board the dog at a kennel, do some research before making your selection. Ask a friend, your veterinarian, or a pet shop proprietor for recommendations. Before dropping the dog off visit the kennel to inspect it for cleanliness and to evaluate the care being given the dogs boarded there already and their current state of health. Also be aware of the kennel's security, as you do not want your dog to be able to escape or perhaps be stolen due to inadequate protection.

All boarding kennels require that the dogs shall have had all necessary immunizations prior to being accepted for boarding. This is to avoid outbreaks of communicable diseases. Upon arrival, inform the proprietor of your dog's medical history and, if he has a medical problem, be sure to leave the appropriate medicine and instructions on how to handle the condition.

Always leave with your dog's caretaker a telephone number where you can be reached, as well as the telephone number of the dog's veterinarian. Try to make the dog feel as much at home as possible before you leave him. Give him his favorite toy or blanket (if this is acceptable to the kennel), as this may help him adjust to the new surroundings.

CARE OF THE OLDER DOG

One of the keys to helping your dog live a long, healthy life is to watch his diet and weight from the time he is a puppy. Do not let him get overweight, as this puts excess strain on the heart and can result in a premature death. Exercise is a necessary requirement throughout his life, but as he ages most vigorous activities should be eliminated to prevent him from overexerting himself. This is especially important in hot weather. Substitute leisurely walks for energetic runs. As the older dog exercises less, his caloric intake should be cut down. Modify his diet as necessary, usually by cutting back his intake by ten to twenty percent.

Painful, arthritic joints are common in the older dog. You can help comfort him by supplying a comfortable bed for him to rest in—perhaps even a waterbed—and try to discourage him from climbing many stairs. Vitamin and mineral supplements have been acclaimed as aids in alleviating joint discomfort. Your veterinarian can advise which vitamins might be useful; perhaps he or she may prescribe medicines that restrict swelling in the joints and relieve pain. Exercise of any kind may be painful, but the arthritic dog must still be encouraged to move about or else the legs will get stiffer and more hurtful, eventually becoming useless. Exercise should, of course, be very moderate. It may also be comforting if you massage the dog's legs once or twice a day to stimulate blood flow and relieve tightness.

The teeth can be a major problem for older dogs. You should regularly check for tartar and remove all build-up. An abscessed tooth is a common malady that often goes undetected until visible signs, such as a purulent wound on the cheek or a loss of appetite, appear. Inspect your dog's mouth and have all diseased teeth removed as soon as they are detected, as infection can result from neglected dental problems.

Nap periods for canine senior citizens may become more frequent and longer, but be alert for signs of continual grogginess. This could be a sign of serious health problems, such as failing kidneys or an overtaxing of the digestive system. A slight increase in his intake of water is to be expected, but drinking excessive amounts of water may be a warning signal of distress. If there is any noticeable change in the dog's behavior, quickly consult your veterinarian or schedule an office visit.

As a dog ages, his eyesight and hearing may become less acute. With this comes an increased chance that the dog may not be able to swiftly respond or react to dangerous situations. Such impaired older dogs must not be allowed free access to the great outdoors. They should be taken out on leash and be more closely monitored than when they were young.

Hearing problems can often be the result of ear mites or an accumulation of excess wax in the ear canal. Left unchecked such conditions can lead to a permanent loss of hearing. However, a thorough cleaning and the administration of some ear medication by a veterinarian can often clear up many hearing disorders in the older dog.

Make life as easy as possible for the infirm older dog by adapting to his needs. Do not change his daily routine, including such minor things as moving his water and food bowls to a new location, unless this is absolutely necessary. Talk to and pet an older dog often to reassure and comfort him.

As the older dog exercises less, his nails get less exposure to the rough surfaces that wear them down. Inspect the nails regularly and trim them when needed. The older dog also needs special care when exposed to the extremes of weather. His coat thins as he ages, so he should be covered with a coat or sweater in cold weather and kept dry to avoid sudden chills. In very hot weather keep him inside as much as possible to avoid heatstroke and dehydration, and provide lots of fresh water. If he appears to be suffering from the heat, a sponge bath with cool water will usually restore his normal body temperature.

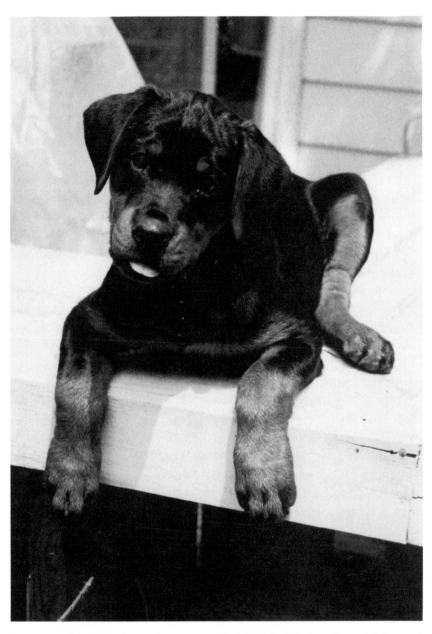

Three-month-old Ch. Inner Sanctums Oh Jezebel, C.D. in a thoughtful pose! Owners: Greg and Lori Benkiser. Young puppies can succumb to all sorts of infectious canine diseases if they are not routinely vaccinated, so as a Rottweiler owner, you must set up an immunization schedule with the veterinarian as soon as possible.

Chapter 5

Health Care

While there are literally thousands of diseases and problems that your dog *can* be subjected to during his lifetime, you should realize that he will most likely live a relatively healthy life. Given the proper blend of exercise, good nutrition, suitable housing, and routine veterinary care, your dog can be expected to be an active member of your household for many years. When it comes to health care, the main point to remember is that you are responsible for noticing any changes in your pet's behavior that may indicate a health problem, but the diagnosis and treatment should be left to a professional—your veterinarian. From the time you first bring the dog into your household you should establish a regular pattern of veterinary visits. In this way your veterinarian gets the chance to become familiar with you and your dog, and the dog receives his necessary inoculations and examinations.

SIGNS OF ILLNESS
Should you notice that your dog is not acting normally, perhaps appearing overly tired and sluggish, review his vital signs. Take his temperature by using a rectal thermometer.

Listlessness is often a sign of fever. Most major ailments cause a rise in temperature above the normal 101° to 102° range. A reading of two degrees above or below the normal is cause for concern and you should consult your veterinarian. A dog's normal pulse rate is from 80 to 140 beats per minute. The pulse is taken from a spot where the artery is near the surface, such as inside the hind leg where the leg meets the body. A very fast pulse can indicate shock, and a weak pulse can indicate a life-threatening condition. A final measure that is easily taken is respiration; a normal rate is from 10 to 30 breaths per minute.

A sudden loss of appetite can be a sign of various ailments: fever, a sore mouth, diseased teeth, or an upset stomach. If it should continue for more than twenty-four hours, a trip to the veterinarian is in order. Likewise with persistent vomiting or diarrhea. While most upsets pass quickly, do not delay in seeking help should your dog pass bloody urine or stools or appear to suffer a seizure.

SUPPLIES

To be prepared for coping with a medical emergency, you should have within easy reach the following items:

- rectal thermometer
- petroleum jelly
- boric acid eyewash
- gauze or cotton bandages
- hydrogen peroxide or iodine
- cotton swabs
- tweezers
- blunt-tipped scissors
- bicarbonate of soda or mineral oil

These supplies can be used as aids in determining the extent of your dog's illness or to handle such minor injuries as cuts, bee stings, or small burns. With minor problems such as these, treat the ailment as you would that of a human. Keep all wounds clean to avoid infection and secure the advice of a veterinarian should there be any signs of complications in healing.

INFECTIOUS DISEASES

Most communicable diseases that dogs are susceptible to can be prevented by obtaining the necessary series of vaccinations during your puppy's initial visits to the veterinarian. During the first weeks of the puppy's life, he receives antibodies from his mother that protect him from disease. Once he is fully weaned, this natural protection is gone and the puppy is vulnerable until he is immunized. Until protected, it is important to keep puppies-at-risk in clean surroundings and limit their contact with other dogs and people who may be carriers of infectious diseases.

The first shots a puppy receives are weak doses that protect for only a short time, so it is vital that two follow-up shots also be administered.Generally a booster will be needed at one year, with yearly shots thereafter. Your veterinarian can set up an immunization schedule for your dog, so discuss this with him as soon as you bring your canine friend into your home. Prevention is the key, as these contagious diseases can be virtually eliminated if proper vaccination procedures are followed throughout your dog's life.

Rabies. This highly contagious viral disease is spread among warm-blooded animals through contact with infectious saliva, and transmission usually occurs by means of an infected animal's bite. The virus travels from the wound site through the central nervous system to the brain where it causes damage and noticeable behavioral changes. Dogs that have not been vaccinated against this dread disease are susceptible,so this is why preventive measures must be taken to ensure your pet is protected. Once a dog is bitten by a rabid animal and clinical signs appear, death soon follows.

The symptoms of rabies generally fall into two classifications. The first is "furious rabies," which begins with a period of depression or melancholy, followed by irritability. In the latter state the dog is most dangerous, as he may be prone to attack other animals or people. These first stages can last several hours to several days. During this time the dog will show little or no interest in eating, change his body position often, lick himself, and try to bite or swallow foreign objects. He becomes spasmodically wild and tries to bite everything around him. If caught and caged at this point, he will relentlessly try to free himself by attacking and biting at the bars that confine him, actions which often result in broken teeth and a fractured jaw. The rabid dog's bark becomes a peculiar howl. The final phase of the disease is marked by a paralysis of the dog's lower jaw which causes it to hang down. Hydrophobia sets in, since the animal is incapable of ingesting water. The dog walks with a stagger, saliva drips from his mouth, and he usually dies within four to eight days after the onset of paralysis.

The second classification of rabies is referred to as "dumb rabies," characterized by the dog's walking in a manner similar to that of a lumbering bear. The head is held down and the jaw is paralyzed. The dog is unable to bite, and he appears to have something caught in the back of his throat.

The only method of prevention is with the appropriate vaccine administered by a veterinarian. Keep in mind that a rabid dog is highly dangerous to humans and other animals; therefore, local public health officials should be contacted even if rabies is suspected. Dogs normally receive their first rabies shot at one year, but it may be administered earlier if the disease is prevalent in a particular municipality. A rabies booster shot, given once every two years, will protect your dog from this deadly disease.

Distemper. Puppies are most prone to contract distemper, which affects the lungs, intestines, and nervous system. It is a deadly disease, but it can be controlled by early inoculation with yearly booster shots reinforcing the protection. Symptoms of the disease are often subtle: loss of appetite and energy, fever and chills, and a discharge from the nose and eyes. If left untreated, the disease quickly intensifies and attacks many major body organs, leaving the dog susceptible to convulsions, paralysis, and death.

Although distemper usually attacks young puppies, dogs of any age can succumb. It is vital that you immunize all young dogs by taking them to the veterinarian at a very early age to protect them when they are most vulnerable, but annual boosters must also be maintained to continue the protection throughout the dog's life.

Leptospirosis. Another disease that can be prevented through proper immunization at an early age is leptospirosis. This disease is caused by rapidly growing bacteria that infect sewage or slow-moving or stagnant water pools. It can be carried by mice or rodents and is most often transmitted when a dog licks substances or objects that have been contaminated by the feces or urine of infected animals.

Symptoms of leptospirosis infection vary and may include: chronic diarrhea; vomiting; fever; depression; a dry coat; and a yellow discoloration of the teeth, tongue, and jaws, which is caused by an acute inflammation of the kidneys. Left unchecked, this disease is deadly, but it is easily controlled through administration of a vaccine (often in conjunction with distemper and hepatitis shots).

Hepatitis. This viral disease is one of the few infectious diseases that has increased in incidence in recent years. Hepatitis is easily spread through casual contact, and young dogs are the most susceptible. Like distemper, the primary symptoms are often subtle: loss of appetite and energy, vomiting, thirst, and fever. Swelling of the abdomen, head, and neck regions is also common. The disease increases in virulence very quickly, and veterinary care is essential as death can occur in just a few hours. Hepatitis can, however, be prevented by a vaccination.

Parainfluenza. This contagious respiratory disease, commonly referred to as *kennel cough*, often attacks whole litters of puppies; in fact, it can devastate entire kennels of dogs. Caused by a virus, the most obvious symptom of this disease is coughing, and a general decline in physical condition follows. An afflicted dog is left very weak and susceptible to other debilitating diseases.

Parainfluenza outbreaks spread very quickly, so it is essential to have all dogs immunized against this deadly disease.

Canine Parvovirus (CPV). This viral disease is not only highly contagious and deadly, but it is often hard to get rid of once an area becomes exposed. The virus is spread chiefly through the feces of infected dogs, and it is capable of existing in the host environment for months at a time. Major disinfection techniques must be applied to rid an afflicted area of the virus.

The incidence of canine parvovirus has been on the increase in recent years, so prevention by means of a vaccination is essential. CPV attacks the intestinal tract, the white blood cells, and often the heart muscle. The symptoms are vomiting, diarrhea or blood-streaked feces, fever, loss of appetite and energy, and dehydration. These symptoms generally appear five to seven days after exposure to the virus. Puppies are the primary victims, as it often proves fatal to young dogs, but older dogs seem to be able to combat the disease more efficiently.

As with most infectious diseases, the best preventative is immunization by the administration of a vaccine by your veterinarian. If you maintain any type of kennel or outdoor housing it is advisable to disinfect the area routinely as a precautionary measure. One part household bleach to thirty parts water can be used effectively. Whenever you take your dog for a walk, do not let him come into contact with the feces of other dogs, as this is a source of CPV infection.

INTERNAL PARASITES

It is very common for dogs, especially when young, to become infected with internal parasites (worms). While most infestations are not severe and are easily cured by medication, if left unchecked worms can cause permanent damage and death. During your puppy's first check-up your veterinarian will look for the presence of worms by examining a stool sample under a microscope. This is the only way to determine exactly which type of parasite, if any, is present.

As your dog ages you should have routine tests for worms performed when he receives his yearly shots. In the time between veterinary visits, be on the lookout for evidence of internal parasites, such as small worms clinging to the dog's bedding, feces, or hair around the anus. He may also "scoot" or drag his backside across the floor (although scooting can also be a sign of overfilled or infected anal glands). If worms are suspected, have your veterinarian perform the necessary diagnostic tests to identify the infestation. *Do not* worm the dog yourself with over-the-counter preparations unless so advised by your veterinarian. This is a common source of accidental poisonings, as dosages in excess of what is recommended are often administered by well-meaning owners.

There are several preventive measures that can be taken to lessen the chances of your dog's becoming infested with internal parasites. A healthy, well-nourished dog is more apt to remain worm-free because of his high stamina than a weak dog. Provide a diet that is high in protein and rich in vitamin A. Proper sanitation is a must. Be sure that the dog's bedding is kept clean and dry to avoid its becoming infested with fleas, ticks, and other external parasites, which are often the carriers of internal parasites.

There are five common types of worms seen in dogs: roundworms, tapeworms, hookworms, whipworms, and heartworms. Because of this diversity, there is no one drug that will cure them all. If these worms are allowed to remain in the dog's system, they will eventually rob the dog of his stamina and produce a general deterioration, loss of weight, diarrhea, dulling of the coat, and vomiting. Due to this weakened condition, the dog also becomes susceptible to other diseases. Two of the most recognizable symptoms are a ravenous appetite without weight gain and a bloating of the stomach.

Roundworms. Roundworms commonly infect puppies, in whom they can cause lung and intestinal damage. The roundworm larvae enter the bloodstream by penetrating the intestinal lining and they are then carried to the lungs. Roundworms can commonly be seen in the feces. Their white cylindrical bodies are pointed at both ends. While they are generally small, they can be thread-like and up to three inches in length. Once roundworms reach the lungs, the dog will have a cough and may be threatened with pneumonia. Roundworms are excreted in the stool and transmitted when a dog comes in contact with contaminated soil. This is why strict sanitation is important so that the cycle of reinfection is broken after treatment for roundworms.

Tapeworms. Fleas, as intermediate hosts, are the most common source of tapeworms in dogs. By eliminating these external parasites, the incidence of tapeworm infestation will be greatly limited. The tapeworm is introduced into the dog's system when the dog bites at and swallows an infected flea or louse. The adult tapeworm attaches itself to the dog's intestinal wall and absorbs nutrients from his system, leaving him very hungry and in a weakened physical condition. Tapeworms may be difficult to eradicate, especially if the head of these segmented parasites remains embedded in the intestinal lining where it can regenerate. Several worming treatments, in this case, may need to be administered by the veterinarian in order to rid your dog of these pests. Over-the-counter tapeworm medications often produce unpleasant side effects, such as vomiting and diarrhea, so be sure to consult your veterinarian for the proper medicine.

Hookworms. If present in large quantities, hookworms can be deadly, as they attach themselves to the wall of the small intestine and, by sucking, remove blood from the dog. If they are left untreated, these bloodsuckers can cause circulatory collapse. Signs of hookworm infestation are diarrhea, anemia, weakness, and weight loss. Hookworms are very small, generally less than one-half inch in length, so detection without laboratory testing is rare. Hookworm larvae generally enter the dog's body by means of his ingesting larval worms off the ground; so, as always, good sanitation will help prevent further infection once treatment has been secured from your veterinarian. This includes properly disposing of all canine fecal matter in which the hookworm eggs have been deposited. Additionally, runs, kennels, and bedding should be disinfected regularly.

Whipworms. Like hookworms, whipworm larvae reach the dog's system through ingestion of larval worms from contaminated soil. In extreme cases symptoms are vomiting, diarrhea, and anemia, but in most cases whipworm infestation is mild and hard to detect. Routine examination for the presence of worms by your veterinarian will help prevent whipworms from going undetected.

Heartworms. The incidence of heartworm infestation in dogs, in the United States especially, has markedly increased in recent years. In its advanced stages, heartworm infestation can be life-threatening, as worms from six to twelve inches in length invade the heart in great numbers. An afflicted dog will have difficulty breathing, cough, tire easily, and lose weight despite a hearty appetite. In advanced cases the heart becomes so clogged with worms that it cannot pump enough blood to the various body organs.

The heartworm parasite is transmitted by mosquitoes who have previously fed off an infected dog. While it was once believed that heartworm infection occurred only in the southern areas of the United States, it has now been proven to occur wherever several species of mosquitoes live—this entails most of the North American continent.

While there is no preventive vaccine for heartworms, they can be avoided by administering daily doses of medication, particularly during the spring, summer, and fall months. If caught in the early stages, heartworm disease can be cured; but it is a slow, uncertain process and prevention by daily pill or liquid medication is strongly advised. The presence of heartworms can be confirmed only by a blood test, so a yearly test (in late winter or early spring, before mosquito season) should be given. The preventive medicine, incidentally, will be prescribed only if the dog proves to be worm-free. If your dog spends much time outdoors during warmer months when mosquitoes abound, it is especially important that you closely monitor him for the onset of heartworms. Early detection is vital.

EXTERNAL PARASITES
External parasites (fleas, ticks, lice, and mites) live on the dog's skin and feed on his blood, tissue fluid, and the skin itself. These parasites may cause irritations to the skin that progress into various infections and disorders. Besides causing problems themselves, some external parasites serve as carriers of disease or hosts for various internal parasites. Fleas, as previously mentioned, often carry tapeworms.

To avoid ectoparasitic infestations on your dog, you must

routinely inspect his skin. Should he become infested, your veterinarian will be able to recommend a medicated shampoo or an appropriate treatment to help eliminate the parasites. The dog's bedding and environment must be cleaned regularly to prevent any embedded eggs from hatching and, thus, reinfecting the dog.

Mange. Parasites are responsible for two types of skin mange: sarcoptic and follicular. Sarcoptic mange is the most common form of this disorder, and it results in an intense skin irritation that causes the dog to scratch violently, often to the point of bloodying the skin. Upon investigation of the irritated skin, the veterinarian will find small red areas that have become engorged with pus. While sarcoptic mange can be controlled and eliminated with medicine provided by your veterinarian, this is a highly contagious condition and the afflicted dog should be kept isolated until he fully recovers.

Follicular mange, while much rarer than sarcoptic mange, is much more difficult to eliminate. The infection of the hair follicles leads to bare patches on the skin. These areas, rather than becoming tender and raw, often become thickened and leathery, which inhibits the hair from growing back in. Follicular mange is less contagious than its counterpart, but it is often a continual problem for an afflicted dog, as it is rarely eliminated in its entirety despite vigilant veterinary attention.

Ear Mites. These parasites live in the ear canal, feeding on skin debris. Signs of ear mites are large deposits of black or reddish brown ear wax, vigorous ear scratching, and head shaking.

Veterinary inspection of the waxy discharge under a microscope will reveal the presence of ear mites. The first step in eliminating the problem is to thoroughly clean the wax from the ear canal. This must be done carefully and should be performed by a trained professional to avoid possible damage to the delicate tissues of the inner ear. If mites are discovered in the wax (wax is also a symptom of other ear disorders), your veterinarian will supply you with medicated ear drops. Through daily application of an ear mite medication, these pesky parasites will be eliminated in several weeks' time.

EMERGENCIES

Accidents, such as being hit by a car, are the most common emergency health situations experienced by dog owners. In an emergency, immediate action is called for to stabilize the injured dog until veterinary care is available. After being hit by a car, a dog should always be examined by a veterinarian for possible internal injuries—even if he appears unhurt.

Cuts, Wounds, and Fractures. In general, primary first aid for a dog is similar to that for a human. When ministering to a dog's wounds, one must be careful to avoid being bitten by the suffering animal. Even a normally docile dog, if painfully injured or badly frightened, is apt to bite anyone who comes near him. Before attempting to care for a severely injured dog in such a state, prepare a muzzle to secure his mouth. A man's necktie or a long strip of cloth will adequately serve this purpose. Begin by placing the midpoint of the cloth across the top of the dog's muzzle, crossing it under the lower jaw, bringing it up around the back of the neck, and tying it in a secure knot just behind and below the ears. This may be frightening to the dog, so talk to him soothingly throughout the procedure.

When dealing with a cut, begin by cleaning the area with a mild soap and hot water to reveal the site. If necessary, trim the hair around the cut so that you can get to the wound. If the wound is large enough to require bandaging, wrap some gauze around the area and get the dog to a veterinarian as soon as possible. Dogs are very adept at removing bandages, so let a professional prepare the dressing.

If the wound is in the head or neck area, you can keep the dog from scratching or licking it by applying an Elizabethan or cone collar. These lightweight collars can be easily constructed to temporarily inhibit the dog from getting to an injury. The collars can be made from cardboard and taped together or bound with thin cord.

Large wounds or ones in which the blood is continuously pouring forth will require pressure to halt the blood flow until veterinary care becomes available. Try to locate a pressure point near the injury to reduce the flow of blood to the area. Take a wad of cotton or a clean cloth and place it over the wound to serve as a pressure bandage. Tightly wrap some gauze over the cotton to hold it in place. In most cases, this should stop the flow of blood; if it doesn't, increase pressure by wrapping the gauze more tightly or by applying adhesive tape tightly over the gauze.

If the bleeding is very severe (perhaps an artery was cut), you will need to devise a tourniquet. Apply a tourniquet between the injury and the heart and twist the bandage until the blood flow is stopped. As with any major injury, time is really of the essence when a tourniquet is applied, as the flow of blood cannot be curtailed to an area for more than ten to fifteen minutes.

When dealing with a seriously injured dog, be sure to keep him as quiet as possible to avoid any further damage to internally injured organs. Talk soothingly and try to keep him as calm as possible. Do not move him unless he is still in danger or unless you need to transport him to a medical professional.

If you suspect that the dog has fractured some bones, restrain him from all movement. If there is a severe or compound fracture (the bone protruding from the wound), you may need to splint the break. In making such a splint, the main point to remember is that you want to keep the area steady, as any movement could cause possible nerve damage by an interruption to the blood supply. Transport the dog to the veterinarian as quickly as possible for immediate treatment.

Poisoning. If you suspect that your dog has swallowed a poisonous substance, first try to locate the source of the poison. If you find the container, read the label for instructions on how to deal with an accidental poisoning. The procedures can vary. To induce vomiting may be the proper treatment in some cases of poisonings, but vomiting may be very damaging in other instances where the proper procedure may be to feed the dog milk or some other substance to help neutralize the poison's effects.

If your dog has been poisoned, you must act quickly. Notify your veterinarian of the problem by phone immediately, giving him as many details as possible so that he can prepare an antidote while you are rushing the dog to his office. He may offer some advice on how to care for the dog during the trip or ask you

This nine-week-old youngster went on to become Ch. Hallmark's "The Sting." A Top Producer for 1983, she went Best of Opposite Sex at Westminster in 1981 and 1982. By Ch. Starkrest's Polo-R ex Ch. Radio Ranch's Echo v. Tanrich. Owners: Patrick and Olga McDonald.

to administer a temporary treatment.

Worming medicines are major causes of poisoning in dogs. Well-meaning owners sometimes medicate their dogs with these preparations as a routine measure. When no worms are expelled, some people figure the dosage was not strong enough so they administer a second, stronger dose. Worming should be undertaken only when an infestation has been confirmed by your veterinarian and only under his guidance.

Other sources of poisonings in dogs are similar to those children often get into: carelessly placed cleaning agents, household products, and plants. Insecticides should be locked away securely. Car antifreeze that has dripped onto the street is surprisingly attractive to dogs, as it gives off a sweet fragrance. Be sure to monitor your dog when walking him to be sure he does not attempt to ingest such a material, as two tablespoons of antifreeze can cause severe kidney damage or death.

Burns. Allowing your dog free run of your house exposes him to many sources of burns: electric shock from biting cords, heat burns from too close contact with a fireplace or heater, or topical burns from overturned pots of hot water or oil in the kitchen.

With heat, or thermal burns, the immediate treatment is to apply cold water or ice compresses to the affected area. Clean the burn site with soap and cool water to remove any contaminants such as hair, dirt, or grass. Then rinse the area well, again with cool water. Avoid exposing the burned skin to the air by covering the area with cotton gauze or a loose bandage. If the burn is very severe, the dog may quickly lapse into shock. Keep him wrapped in a blanket and try to soothe him and keep him still while you get veterinary assistance.

Electric shock burns can be confined strictly to the mouth or they may affect the entire system. Only a veterinarian can properly handle such a situation, so contact him immediately and take the dog to him as quickly as possible. Even if the shock seems minor, there may be some damage to the mouth region that will require medication.

Insect Bites or Stings. While most insect bites are inconsequential and unknown to the dog owner, occasionally your dog may have an allergic reaction to a sting. This will generally be manifest in an outbreak of hives or other bumps on the skin. In minor cases such as this, examine the site of the sting and remove the stinger if you can find it.

In many rare cases your dog may have a severe reaction to the toxin from the sting. Danger signals are extreme swelling of the affected area and difficulty in breathing. Such a reaction is life-threatening and a veterinarian should be immediately contacted, as corticosteroids or other anti-inflammation drugs may need to be administered to halt the progression of the allergic reaction. Reactions such as this often follow a sting that occurred from the dog's snapping at and catching a bee or wasp in his mouth. Be alert to the possibility of such a dangerous sting if your dog is prone to this kind of behavior and correct him whenever you see him trying to catch insects. Keep in mind though that this natural instinct is hard to break.

Heatstroke. Heatstroke occurs most often in dogs that have been confined to a car or other small enclosure without proper ventilation on a warm day. It does not have to be 90 °F outside for heatstroke to occur. A parked, poorly ventilated car can reach 100 °F in a short amount of time on a relatively mild 75 °F day. If you must leave your dog in the car for any reason, be sure to lower several windows at least three inches, leave a supply of water, and *make the confinement short.* If the dog is going to have to remain confined for any length of time, do everyone a favor and leave him home or take him along with you when you leave the car.

A change of climate can also induce heatstroke. Bringing a dog from a mild weather area to a hot climate without giving him time to adjust can put the dog into extreme physical stress. Very young or old dogs, as well as overweight dogs, are susceptible to heat stroke if they are allowed to exert themselves on hot days.

Panting is the most obvious sign of heat stress. If this is coupled with an increased heart rate, agitation, and/or vomiting, contact your veterinarian immediately. He will probably advise you to take the dog's temperature rectally. If it is substantially elevated, he may have to be immersed in cool water immediately to break the upward progression of his temperature. If left unchecked, the dog can go into circulatory collapse and die. Treatment by your veterinarian will be required in all heat stress cases, as there are often secondary reactions that follow the initial temperature elevation.

Heatstroke can almost always be avoided by following some common sense rules. Always have a plentiful supply of water on hand, especially when travelling or on very hot days. Encourage your dog to take frequent small drinks. If you must place your dog in a carrier or confined area, supply him with some wet towels to help cool the area by evaporation. Never allow the dog to overtax his system on a hot day, and take special care of overweight, old, or very young dogs. These dogs should be kept inside, out of the sun, if at all possible.

Snakebite. If your dog should tangle with a snake, first try to determine whether the snake was poisonous. Two fang marks usually indicate a poisonous bite, while a U-shaped row of teeth marks usually indicates a nonpoisonous bite. Should your dog be bitten by a poisonous snake, immediate action must be taken or paralysis and death can quickly follow. The first step is to calm and immobilize the dog, as exertion will further spread the venom in the dog's system. Such bites are very painful, so before you attempt to medicate your dog, muzzle him to prevent being bitten.

If the snakebite is on a leg, apply a tourniquet between the wound and the heart. It is not necessary to completely shut down the flow of blood, as with a severely bleeding wound, but to slow it dramatically. If possible, try to keep the bitten limb on a level that is horizontal with the heart to slow the movement of the venom through the bloodstream. If a veterinarian can reach the dog within ten minutes of the bite, this tourniquet generally will be enough to sustain him until the doctor can treat the wound and administer an antitoxin.

If there is no immediate veterinary attention available, you will need to open up the bite wound and try to remove as much of the poison from the area as possible. Use a sterilized sharp instrument (a knife or razor blade) and make two linear incisions above and below the wound to start the blood flowing. Apply suction (preferably not by mouth but with a suction cup) and get the dog to a veterinarian immediately. The dog will need immediate antitoxin, antibiotics, and pain killers.

Fire. Fire and smoke are life-threatening conditions for man and dog alike, and immediate evacuation from the burning area is the solution. However, many fires can occur when the owner is not at home and the dog is confined to the house or in a crate. Firemen will be unaware of the dog's presence unless they are alerted to it. Conscientious owners should post a decal in a prominent window that specifies the number of pets on the premises and the approximate area in which they can be found.

HEALTH DISORDERS

Dogs, like man, are susceptible to various disorders that can affect their quality of life. Advances in medicine and health care in recent years have gone far in increasing the knowledge of trained professionals in how to prevent, treat, and cure many of the most prevalent conditions.

Respiratory Infections. While viruses and bacteria are the true causes of such complaints as colds, bronchitis, and pneumonia, exposure to a draft after a bath, allowing a dog to sleep in the path of an air conditioner's current or near a radiator, and subjecting the dog to frequent temperature changes are man-made conditions that can affect the dog's overall health.

Sneezing, fever, water or pussy eyes, and a lack of appetite are common symptoms of respiratory infections. Mild cases involving a moderate amount of sneezing and a little eye discharge can generally be treated by keeping the dog warm, well-fed and watered, and inactive. If the discharges become pus-like and there are accompanying signs of dehydration, lack of appetite, and a persistent fever, veterinary care is in order. Antibiotics will generally be prescribed to counter the effect of the invading germs.

Constipation. While mild, temporary constipation can occur naturally in the dog due to changes in diet or as a reaction to cold, rainy weather (when the dog's thoughts are not on elimination out-of-doors but on getting back into the warmth of the house), severe straining or a continued lack of bowel movements can indicate serious health problems, such as a tumor or an obstruction in the intestines.

If the condition seems mild, try increasing the amount of roughage in the dog's diet or add a small amount of mineral oil to his food once a day. The mineral oil supplements should not, however, be continued for more than three days, as the oil may interfere with the body's natural absorption of vitamins and minerals.

In more severe cases, consult your veterinarian. He may suggest such remedies as administering a mild dose of milk of magnesia as a laxative, or he may prescribe glycerine suppositories or an enema of warm water and mild soap.

Urine retention can also become a life-threatening condition if toxic substances are allowed to build up in the bladder and

ORTHOPEDIC FOUNDATION FOR ANIMALS INC.

JENEK'S MANDY
registered name of dog

ROTTWEILER
breed

BLACK AND TAN
color

---
tattoo

138786
application number

APRIL 1, 1982
date of report

---
registration number (AKC, CKC)

FEMALE
sex

MARCH 3, 1980
date of birth

24
age at evaluation in months

RO-3340
OFA registry number

The registry number issued with the right to correct or revoke by the Orthopedic Foundation for Animals.

BASED UPON THE RADIOGRAPH SUBMITTED THE CONSENSUS WAS THAT NO EVIDENCE OF HIP DYSPLASIA WAS RECOGNIZED.

THE HIP JOINT CONFORMATION WAS EVALUATED AS: **EXCELLENT**

E. A. CORLEY, D.V.M.
PROJECT DIRECTOR

DYSPLASIA CONTROL REGISTRY

owner

VIVIAN A. PETERS
6220 JAPATUL HIGHLANDS ROAD
ALPINE, CA 92001

DENEL'S MONA LISA
registered name of dog

ROTTWEILER
breed

BLACK & RUST
color

DECEMBER 22, 1982
date of report

WF-188805
registration no.

FEMALE
sex

---
tattoo

owner
VIVIAN A. PETERS
6220 JAPATUL HIGHLANDS RD.
ALPINE, CA 92001

veterinarian
BROADWAY ANIMAL HOSPITAL
380 BROADWAY
EL CAJON, CA 92021

RADIOGRAPHIC EVALUATION OF PELVIC PHENOTYPE WITH RESPECT TO CANINE HIP DYSPLASIA

Consultation by: E. A. Corley, D.V.M.   Age at evaluation _____ 14 _____ months

_____ **EXCELLENT HIP JOINT CONFORMATION**
superior hip joint conformation as compared with other individuals of
the same breed and age

✓ **GOOD HIP JOINT CONFORMATION**
well formed hip joint conformation as compared with other individuals
of the same breed and age

_____ **FAIR HIP JOINT CONFORMATION**
minor irregularities of hip joint conformation as compared with other
individuals of the same breed and age

_____ **BORDERLINE HIP JOINT CONFORMATION**
marginal hip joint conformation of indeterminate status with respect to
hip dysplasia at this time

_____ **MILD HIP DYSPLASIA**
radiographic evidence of minor dysplastic change of the hip joints

_____ **MODERATE HIP DYSPLASIA**
well defined radiographic evidence of dysplastic changes of
the hip joints

_____ **SEVERE HIP DYSPLASIA**
radiographic evidence of marked dysplastic changes of the hip joints

*The radiograph submitted of the dog described in this report was referred to a veterinary radiologist for his opinion because the film did not meet one or more of the requirements for the formal certification program. The radiograph will be returned to the referring veterinarian under separate cover.

RADIOGRAPHIC FINDINGS

HIP JOINTS - STANDARD VD VIEW
_____ subluxation
_____ remodeling of femoral head/neck
_____ osteoarthritis/degenerative joint disease
_____ shallow acetabula
_____ acetabular rim/edge change
_____ unilateral pathology

ELBOW JOINTS - FLEXED LATERAL VIEW
_____ negative for elbow dysplasia ___ L ___ R
_____ ununited anconeal process ___ L ___ R
_____ osteoarthritis/degenerative joint disease

STIFLE JOINTS - VD VIEW
_____ medial patellar luxation
_____ osteoarthritis degenerative joint disease
_____
_____

SPINE, SACRUM, TAIL - VD VIEW
_____ spondylosis
_____ transitional vertebra
_____

MISCELLANEOUS - VD VIEW
_____ previous fracture
_____ soft tissue calcification
_____ foreign body
_____

Above and facing page are examples of OFA certification and hip evaluation. A dog must be two years old to have its hips certified but it can have its hips *evaluated* prior to that time.

kidneys. If this condition continues for more than twenty-four hours, consult your veterinarian.

Hip Dysplasia. While this disorder is most common in the larger dog breeds, it can be found to affect all breeds. Hip dysplasia (HD) is a misalignment of the bones of the hip: the femur and the acetabulum. Generally, one of these bones is malformed and the surrounding tissues and ligaments cannot hold the bones in place. Either the acetabulum (socket) is too shallow and therefore cannot retain the head of the femur, causing slippage; or the head of the femur is flattened, which causes it to slip from the socket. The end result of this misfit is a stiffness in the rear legs and pain in movement.

Hip dyspasia exists in varying degrees of severity and is generally believed to be hereditary. While the condition is as yet incurable and uncorrectable by surgery, there is considerable study underway on how to eliminate this crippling disease. Medicines to alleviate the pain and reduce some of the inflammation and thereby allow the dog to move more naturally are available through veterinarians.

HD usually begins to noticeably affect a dog by two to six months of age. A dog displaying symptoms of HD should be X-rayed to determine the extent to which he is afflicted. Any dog that is diagnosed as having HD should never be used as breeding stock, as he can pass the disease along to his progeny. To avoid a deterioration of the hip joint, it is also advised that the dog be restricted from climbing stairs and partaking in vigorous exercise, especially while growing, as this may increase the degeneration of the hip joints.

Eczema. Unlike other skin ailments, eczema is generally caused by improper nutrition rather than by a parasite. Eczema causes skin irritation and lesions to appear primarily along the back, especially in the tail region. It occurs mostly in the summer during hot, humid weather when the growth of bacteria is encouraged. A dog in a weakened condition is very susceptible to the invasion of this bacteria. The condition manifests itself in a small lesion, which the dog proceeds to spread by incessant scratching. Eczema is so irritating to the dog that he may scratch at himself until the lesion becomes bloody and raw. An antibiotic ointment will be needed to kill the bacteria and to relieve the itching. It is also advised to keep the dog free of fleas so that he won't scratch himself and in so doing spread the disease. A mild tranquilizer may have to be administered to control the frantic scratching.

A variant form of eczema called "hot spots" or "weeping mange" produces a moist infection and spreads very rapidly. It is not confined to the back and may infect many parts of the body. Along with the general symptoms of intense itching and bacterial infection may come vomiting, engorgement of the lymph nodes, and fever. An emollient to relieve itching and prevent further damage to the skin by scratching must be applied to the affected area after it has been thoroughly cleaned and clipped bare of fur. Your veterinarian will also prescribe an antibiotic and possibly an anti-inflammatory drug if the moist eczema has become severe.

Diabetes. As with humans, diabetes is a condition where there is an imbalance between the amount of sugar in the bloodstream and the amount of insulin that is produced to regulate the sugar usage. Because of the dog's inability to produce a sufficient amount of insulin, an excess amount of sugar remains in the blood. Symptoms are excessive thirst, weight loss, and frequent urination.

If left unchecked, diabetes can be fatal; however, great advances in curing this disease have taken place in recent years. Until a cure is perfected, there are very effective ways of controlling the disease. In severe cases insulin injections are prescribed, but in many instances close regulation of the diet can keep the diabetes under control.

TOOTH CARE

If tartar, or plaque, is allowed to build up at the gum line of your dog's teeth, this scaly deposit will eventually erode the tooth enamel, push the gums away from the teeth, and cause the teeth to loosen and fall out. To avoid such disastrous problems, periodically check the dog's teeth for signs of tartar. If you should notice a mild build-up of this material, brush his teeth once a week with a paste made from bicarbonate of soda and a little hydrogen peroxide. Apply the paste with a child's toothbrush or a gauze pad.

If the dog is prone to heavy tartar build-up, scraping the teeth will be necessary. This is best handled by your veterinarian, who may instruct you on how to carry this out at home if he feels this is a continuous problem.

If your dog develops offensive breath, this may be a sign of dirty or decaying teeth or diseased tonsils. If this condition persists for more than a few days, consult your veterinarian. A dental checkup is also in order if your dog shows a disinterest in eating for more than two days or if there are signs of redness, swelling, or sensitivity on the gums or in and around the mouth.

As with humans, a dog needs his teeth throughout his life. Take special care not to let them deteriorate unnecessarily or let them be injured through roughhousing. An easy way to wear off the points of your dog's teeth is to throw stones or other solid materials for your dog to retrieve. Specially designed toys and balls for dogs are the only items you should use for this type of game.

ALL DOGS NEED TO CHEW

Puppies and young dogs need something with resistance to chew on while their teeth and jaws are developing—for cutting the puppy teeth, to induce growth of the permanent teeth under the puppy teeth, to assist in getting rid of the puppy teeth at the proper time, to help the permanent teeth through the gums, to assure normal jaw development and to settle the permanent teeth solidly in the jaws.

The adult dog's desire to chew stems from the instinct for tooth cleaning, gum massage and jaw exercise—plus the need for an outlet for periodic doggie tensions.

This is why dogs, especially puppies and young dogs, will often destroy property worth hundreds of dollars, when their chewing instinct is not diverted from their owner's possessions, particularly during the widely varying critical period for young dogs.

Saving your possessions from destruction, assuring proper development of teeth and jaws, providing for 'interim' tooth cleaning and gum massage, and channeling doggie tensions into a non-destructive outlet are, therefore, all dependent upon the dog having something suitable for chewing readily available when his instinct tells him to chew. If your purposes, and those of your dog, are to be accomplished, what you provide for chewing must be desirable from the doggie viewpoint, have the necessary functional qualities, and above all, be safe for your dog.

It is very important that dogs not be permitted to chew on anything they can break, or indigestible things from which they can bite sizeable chunks. Sharp pieces, such as from a bone which can be broken by a dog, may pierce the intestine wall and kill. Indigestible things which can be bitten off in chunks, such as toys made of rubber compound or cheap plastic, may cause an intestinal stoppage, if not regurgitated—to bring painful death, unless surgery is promptly performed.

Strong natural bones, such as 4 to 8 inch lengths of round shin bone from mature beef—either the kind you can get from your butcher or one of the variety available commercially in pet stores—may serve your dog's teething needs, if his mouth is large enough to handle them effectively.

You may be tempted to give your puppy a smaller bone and he may not be able to break it when you do—but puppies grow rapidly and the power of their jaws constantly increases until maturity. This means that a growing dog may break one of the smaller bones at any time, swallow the pieces and die painfully before you realize what is wrong.

Many people make the mistake of thinking of their dog's teeth in terms of the teeth of the wild carnivores or those of the dog in antiquity. The teeth of the wild carnivorous animals, and the teeth found in the fossils of the dog-like creatures of antiquity, have far thicker and stronger enamel than those of our contemporary dogs.

All hard natural bones are highly abrasive. If your dog is an avid chewer, natural bones may wear away his teeth prematurely; hence, they then should be taken away from your dog when the teething purposes have been served. The badly worn, and usually painful, teeth of many mature dogs can be traced to excessive chewing on natural bones.

Contrary to popular belief, knuckle bones which can be chewed up and swallowed by the dog provide little, if any, useable calcium or other nutriment. They do, however, disturb the digestion of most dogs and cause them to vomit the nourishing food they need.

An old leather shoe is a popular answer to the chewing need—but be very sure that the rubber heel, all nails, and other metal parts such as lace grommets, metal arches, etc., have been removed. Be especially careful to get all of the nails. A chunk of rubber heel can cause an intestinal stoppage. If it has a nail in it, the intestine wall may be pierced or torn. Then there is, of course, always the hazard that your dog may fail to differentiate between his shoe and yours, and eat up a good pair while you're not looking.

Dried rawhide products of various types, shapes, sizes and prices are available on the market and have become quite popular. However, they don't serve the primary chewing functions very well; they are a bit messy when wet from mouthing, and most dogs chew them up rather rapidly—but they have been considered safe for dogs until recently. Now, more and more incidents of death, and near death, by strangulation have been reported to be the result of partially swallowed chunks of rawhide swelling in the throat. More recently, some veterinarians have been attributing cases of acute constipation to large pieces of incompletely digested rawhide in the intestine.

The nylon bones, especially those with natural meat and bone fractions added, are probably the most complete, safe and economical answer to the chewing need. Dogs cannot break them or bite off sizeable chunks; hence, they are completely safe—and being longer lasting than other things offered for the purpose, they are economical.

70

Hard chewing raises little bristle-like projections on the surface of the nylon bones—to provide effective interim tooth cleaning and vigorous gum massage, much in the same way your tooth brush does it for you. The little projections are raked off and swallowed in the form of thin shavings—but the chemistry of the nylon is such that they break down in the stomach fluids and pass through without effect.

The toughness of the nylon provides the strong chewing resistance needed for important jaw exercise and effective help for the teething functions—but there is no tooth wear because nylon is so non-abrasive. Being inert, nylon does not support the growth of microorganisms—and it can be washed in soap and water, or it can be sterlized by boiling or in an autoclave.

Nylabone® is highly recommended by veterinarians as a safe, healthy nylon bone that can't splinter or chip. Instead, Nylabone is frizzled by the dog's chewing action, creating a toothbrush-like surface that cleanses the teeth and massages the gums. Nylabone® and Nylaball®, the only chew products made of flavor-impregnated solid nylon, are available in your local pet shop.

Nothing, however, substitutes for periodic professional attention to your dog's teeth and gums, not any more than your toothbrush can do that for you. Have your dog's teeth cleaned by your veterinarian at least once a year, twice a year is better—and he will be healthier, happier and far more pleasant to live with.

Am. and Can. Ch. Donnaj Vt Yankee of Paulus, C.D.X., TT by Ch. Axel vom Schwanenschlag ex Ch. Amsel von Andan, C.D. Yankee was the No. 1 Top Producer of champions for 1980 and 1982 and a Top Producer for 1983. He is the sire of 35 champions including 13 Group placers. Bred by Pauline Rakowski and owned by Jan Marshall.

Chapter 6

Breeding the Rottweiler

I would like to begin this chapter with a strong caveat: unless you are completely committed to the Rottweiler breed and are prepared to make sacrifices for it, you would be better off not getting into the breeding aspect of the dog game. Oh, to be sure, it can be a most compelling hobby for those who have been bitten by the "bug" of trying to produce the perfect Rottweiler. Unfortunately, too many people may be tempted to breed dogs—the Rottweiler in particular—because the breed currently commands such high prices. It needs to be pointed out, however, that dogs are like rabbits, in that they can reproduce rapidly. Thus, if a large number of people get into breeding the dogs strictly for profit, the demand for Rotts will be exceeded, and many people will be "stuck" with excess pups. Worse, the people who breed pups for profit will most likely not want to incur much expense, either for the bitch or the stud fee. Thus, deterioration in the breed that we spoke of earlier is a result of all this indiscriminate breeding that is seemingly the inevitable result of a breed being popular, being in demand, and commanding high prices.

Besides, there are many disadvantages to breeding dogs. For one thing, most people are interested in the dog game because they are dog lovers, and yet the selective breeding of dogs consists, partly, of breeding a number of animals and selecting the very cream of the crop, perhaps less than ten percent, for brood stock. The rest must be sterilized, placed in good homes (not an easy proposition for a grown dog—especially a kennel-raised dog), or euthanized. Now, we're talking about dogs that you have raised up to a point at which a fault of some kind surfaces. Other than that one fault, possibly one of temperament but more likely a physical one, the dog is the same animal with the same charm that he was before the fault became known. But because of the fault, he (or she) must be culled, regardless of other obvious traits. Welcome to the harsh world of selective breeding! That doesn't mean that people who do selective breeding are monsters. In fact, such people have a noble purpose in mind: the preservation and improvement of a valued breed. No attempt here is made to denigrate such efforts. I merely wish to point out that there is a dark side to selective breeding. In fact, an old saying among breeders is "He who will not drown, must not breed." The saying refers to the drowning of puppies because they are the "wrong" color or have a physical defect at even this young age. Now I have been advised by breeders—good people, not bad people—that it is impossible to put a puppy in the water bucket and leave it there unless you walk away without looking back. To me, drowning a puppy is like drowning a baby, and I doubt very much I could do it. Yet, I have been bitten by the selective-breeding bug, and therefore I am foresworn to cull out unfit stock. Fortunately, I have had very few pups that needed euthanasia for any reason, and since I have a background in chemistry and biology, I could utilize sodium pentathol, if I had to, to provide a comfortable end. Nevertheless, I have also paid high veterinary bills for the euthanization of animals that I couldn't put to sleep myself.

An important message to get across is that there is very little long-term profit in breeding dogs—of any breed. There are exceptions that prove the rule, but these operate under unusual circumstances or as a result of good fortune, whereby everything breaks exactly right. Anyway, the point is that there is very little *real* profit in breeding dogs, so even those who are involved in that activity strictly for profit, and thereby do so much harm to purebred dogs, are not likely to experience financial gain. Ironically, the ones who buy cheap brood stock, sell a number of litters, and then get out of the business before their reputations as peddlers of unsound dogs catch up to them are the ones most likely to achieve financial gain.

So, we have a heavy moral decision to make before we enter into the selective breeding hobby. And, keeping in mind that there is an overpopulation of dogs in the United States that results in tens of thousands being put to death *daily*, the decision to breed should not be taken lightly. One must have tremendous commitment to the breed. If you think in terms of such commitment, concern for the kinds of homes your potential puppies will receive automatically comes to mind. First of all, raising pups up to eight weeks of age produces an attachment to them in all but the most callous of humans. It is bad enough to have to give them up at all, but then you have to worry about the kinds of homes they will get. Just the fact that a person can afford to buy a pup doesn't mean that he will be a good, responsible, and understanding dog owner. Not only do you worry about the individual pup, but you are also concerned about the reputation of the breed, for an irresponsible dog owner can cause people around him to have ill feelings toward any breed of dog. One solution to this particular problem, however, is a "seller's contract" that spells out your responsibilities as the seller, but it should also include basic minimum care and training that the buyer agrees to provide.

REWARDS OF SELECTIVE BREEDING

Many will feel that I have been unduly dismal about the idea of entering into the hobby of selectively breeding dogs, but I think the disadvantages of the activity are too seldom pointed out (and I didn't even mention the problem of being tied down to the number of dogs that it takes to maintain a successful breeding program). Some of the people who enjoy purebred dogs the most are those who obtain only one or, at the most, two dogs and devote all their free time to training and other activities that allow the dog to become all that his genes allow. Still, selective breeding has its rewards, although they are often ephemeral. For one thing, if you do manage to produce that once-in-a-lifetime dog, the thrill of the accomplishment almost makes it all worthwhile. Further, if you produce an unusually good-producing stud dog or brood bitch, you will be assured of at least a small spot in the breed's history. And if you produce a line of consistently good dogs, people may even say nice things about you! In fact, you may become a minor "cult hero" of sorts in the dog game. Ironically, though, the way to attain that goal is to be thinking not about personal glory, but rather, to be thinking constantly about the welfare of the breed and to let that consideration guide all your transactions and your breedings.

Besides whatever public glory you may obtain, it is quite rewarding to have the personal satisfaction in knowing that you have helped eliminate certain defects or diseases from your breed, or at least a line of your breed. In order to do this, it is necessary to resort to a type of breeding that is almost universally condemned by those who don't know very much about genetics, and that is inbreeding.

PEDIGREES

A dog's pedigree can be an effective tool in aiding a breeder to produce better dogs—if enough is known about the dog's ancestors to supply information on their genetic makeup, that is. This is one reason why it is strongly suggested that if you are interested in breeding you purchase the best quality specimen possible from an established kennel. Because established breeders tend to keep exacting records of their matings and puppies, you should be able to find information about the strengths and weaknesses of your dog's descendants—if you are willing and interested enough to search and ask questions.

When you purchased your puppy, you may have been given a copy of your dog's pedigree. If not, most breeders would be hap-

Ch. V. Gailingen's Welkerhaus Cia, C.D. pictured at four-and-a-half years of age. Breeder: Catherine M. Thompson. Owner: Rita Welker.

py to supply you with one if it is requested. Most pedigrees go back three generations, and these are all you need to concern yourself with. Ancestors beyond the third generation have little influence on your dog. Some people feel that a five-generation pedigree is valuable as it contains information on sixty dogs. This listing of your dog's close relatives can tell you more than just the names of his ancestors. It can also indicate the breeding strategies (linebreeding, inbreeding, outcrossing, outbreeding) followed by the breeder.

When investigating your dog's pedigree, bear in mind that while the names of champions may appear throughout your dog's ancestry, this is no guarantee that the offspring will be of superior quality. Show-quality dogs often produce pet-quality progeny. The traits transmitted to a puppy depend on the genetic structure that he inherits from his parents and their parents before him. To understand the factor of probability involved in breeding dogs, it is strongly suggested that a prospective breeder have a working knowledge of genetic principles and how they relate to dog breeding.

THE MECHANICS OF GENETICS

The passage of traits or characteristics from parent to off-spring does not occur in a haphazard manner. It is a matter of genetic inheritance. The science of genetics traces back to the work of an Austrian monk named Gregor Mendel who discovered that there is a reliable method of inheritance that can be predicted. Mendel found that small units, called *genes,* are present in the cells of all individuals. These genes control the development of the organism's characteristics. They are present in pairs, with one half of each pair being inherited from each parent. When each half of the partner genes was found to affect the organism in an identical manner, the pair was called *homozygous.* When each half of the pair was found to affect the organism in a contrasting manner, the pair was called *heterozygous.*

Mendel discovered that in heterozygous gene pairs containing contrasting characteristics, one half of the pair suppresses the characteristics contained in the other half of the pair. He termed the characteristic that expresses itself *dominant,* and the one that remained hidden he termed *recessive.* There are instances, however, when neither gene is completely dominant over the other. This is known as *incomplete or partial dominance* and the result is a blending of the characteristics from the pair. A few examples of traits that are genetically dominant and recessive in dogs are as follows:

Dominant	Recessive
Dark eyes.	Light eyes
Brown eyes	Blue eyes
Short coat	Long coat
Wire coat	Smooth coat
Curly coat	Straight coat
Large ears	Small ears
Long ears	Short ears
Low set ears	High set ears
Erect ears	Dropped ears
High set tail	Low set tail

Black nose	Dudley nose
Short foreface	Long foreface
Long head	Short head

To put these principles to work in breeding better dogs, breeders must understand that what a dog looks like physically, or on the outside, does not directly·reflect what he looks like genetically, on the inside. His outward appearance is his *phenotype*, and all the traits he has inherited from his ancestors that he can pass on to his offspring form his *genotype*. Phenotype is not a guarantee of genotype. In other words, what a dog looks and acts like is no guarantee that he can pass these traits on to his offspring. This is even further complicated by the fact that some traits (phenotypes) are the result of several genes and therefore difficult to predict.

1. Two dominant genes: he is pure for that trait, having received a dominant gene from each parent. This is termed *dominant/homozygous*.
2. Two recessive genes: he is pure for that trait, having received a recessive gene from each parent. This is termed *recessive/homozygous*.
3. One dominant and one recessive gene: he is mixed for that trait, having received a dominant gene from one parent and a recessive gene from the other. This is termed *heterozygous*.

By applying these (simplified) principles, there is a ratio that can be applied to help predict the genotype of the offspring of a mating. If a parent is homozygous for a trait (1 and 2), he will pass on that trait regardless of which half of his gene pair he gives to the offspring. If a parent is heterozygous for a trait (3), he will pass on either a dominant or a recessive gene to his offspring—a 50/50 chance. These ratios apply for both parents, and whether or not an offspring exhibits a trait depends on the number of dominant and recessive genes he receives from each half of the inherited gene pairs. There are six ways that a pair of

79

genes can unite, based on the possible combinations of dominance and recessiveness present in the genotype of the sire and dam.

The task facing a dedicated breeder is to determine what genes are present in his breeding stock and to plan matings that will bring forth offspring which exhibit and carry desirable genes. The goal is to eliminate unwanted traits not only from the phenotype but also from the genotype of future generations. In this way the overall quality of the breed should improve. The breeding out of undesirable characteristics can be successful if sires and dams are selected carefully, using various breeding strategies to find mates that complement each other. It is important to choose a mate who shows strengths where his partner shows weaknesses, an animal whose background is compatible with that of his partner's.

Linebreeding. This is the process whereby dogs of fairly close relationship are mated in order to eliminate faults and "fix" a uniform type in the offspring by increasing the homozygosity of the gene pairs. Linebreeding usually involves mating dogs that share a common ancestor but that are not closely related themselves. The potential sire and dam should both contain a common ancestor in their second or third generation. This ancestor should be of superior quality, known to pass on his quality to his offspring. Through linebreeding correct type is set and maintained through several generations, and it is the system most recommended by experienced breeders.

Inbreeding. This is a strategy whereby closely related dogs are mated: dam to son, sire to daughter, brother to sister, or half-brother to half-sister. This system is generally used only by experienced breeders who have a good knowledge of the genotypes of the dogs being considered for a mating and know that certain genes are present that they want to concentrate in the offspring. It is also used to expose faults in the breeding line and thereby eliminate them (by eliminating the carriers) from further matings. Because this system concentrates and fixes type very quickly, inferior pups are often produced that must be culled.

80

This system should not be employed very often; when it is, it should not be used by novices.

Outcrossing. Unlike linebreeding, which tries to increase the homozygosity of the gene pairs, outcrossing is a system by which new genes are introduced to increase the heterozygosity of the gene pool. To accomplish this, mates are selected that complement each other while not sharing any common ancestors within at least the last five generations. The breeder is deliberately attempting to add some new, desirable trait or traits to compensate for qualities that are lacking in his breeding stock. The sire or dam selected for the outcross should most likely be the product of linebreeding and thereby exhibit strong prepotency for the traits needed in the breeding program. Outcrossing should be attempted only sparingly, when a specific need is quoted in the breeding program. Once outcrossing is accomplished, breeders generally breed the offspring to a linebreeding plan.

Outbreeding. This is really the unsystematic approach to breeding, the pattern followed by most well-meaning novices who mate their purebred dogs to any available purebred that is easily accessible. Often the ancestry of the sire and dam are unknown and they most likely share no common relatives. There is a high level of heterozygosity and the offspring are generally genetically inferior specimens. Outbreeding should not be confused with crossbreeding, which is the mating of distinct breeds—the products of which are mongrels. Outbreeding rarely produces show-quality animals and does little for the breed except bring forth puppies. As there is generally an overabundance of such puppies, outbreeding is the system knowledgeable breeders would most like eliminated.

THE ADVANTAGES OF INBREEDING
If inbreeding is such a valuable tool, why does it have such a bad name? Why are so many faults attributed to too much inbreeding? Well, among wild populations of living things, and we'll include humans in this cateogry, inbreeding *is* undesirable. The reason is that inbreeding tends to limit the variation of

genetic traits, and that is definitely undesirable in a population that should be able to make small, or major, evolutionary changes in response to changes in the environment. With an artificial variety, such as a dog breed, we don't worry about lack of uniformity; in fact, uniformity, in at least some traits, is exactly what we seek. We want Rottweilers to look like Rottweilers and not like a group of mongrels. So inbreeding is useful to provide us with uniformity. (It is worth mentioning here, however, that not all purebred breeds are bred for uniformity of appearance. To take just one example, the marvellous Border Collie is bred strictly for herding ability. Connoisseurs of the breed do not want a standard; in fact, they argue mightily against the idea of one. The uniformity in that breed does still exist, but it consists of behavioral traits that make it the top herding dog in the world.)

Besides "fixing" desired traits in a breed and providing uniformity in the desired areas, inbreeding also brings out faults. It doesn't produce the faults or diseases, but it brings them to the surface. The reason for this phenomenon is that, quite simply, when you reduce the variation of your basic gene pool, the recessives, including the desirable as well as the undesirable, are going to be paired and, thus, appear more often in the individual dogs. However, a strain may be purified of these undesirable traits by continuing to inbreed and culling out the individuals with the undesirable traits (e.g., hip dysplasia). It is an expensive proposition, but a breeder who sticks to a pure line and purifies it of all the undesirable traits and diseases that are extant in a given breed ends up with a very valuable and highly-respected line of dogs.

In addition to "cleansing" a line of faults and giving it uniformity, inbreeding helps produce very prepotent stud dogs. That is, the dogs tend to produce better than "scatter-bred" or outcrossed dogs. The same is true of bitches, too, of course. There are several problems with inbreeding, and it should only be undertaken by a breeder who has studied the situation and understands what he is doing. One of the problems is that by staying within an inbred line, you limit your choices of what you breed to, as a simple matter of numbers. Hence, a program based on inbreeding must start with very outstanding foundation stock, and selectivity must be uncompromising.

Actually, uncompromising selectivity is the primary key to *any* breeding program, as breeders have been successful utilizing inbreeding, linebreeding, and outcrossing. However, it has been argued that there is no such thing as a legitimate outcross in a purebred dog. I tend to agree with that view, strictly speaking; however, when we use these terms, we are speaking in a relative sense. Normally, inbreeding is considered to be breeding anything closer than cousins. However, Kyle Onstott has pointed out, quite correctly, that cousins can be more closely related (more common ancestors, more common genetic material) than brother and sister. At the very least, this possibility is true on a hypothetical basis. However, brother to sister is considered the closest inbreeding, and each parent is considered half-brother to its offspring. Linebreeding is generally considered to be mating related individuals that are beyond first cousins. And, of course, outbreeding is the mating of completely unrelated individuals. We have already spoken of this situation as being basically non-existent with purebred dogs; however, most breeders (and geneticists) would consider the breeding of two dogs with no common ancestors in a five-generation pedigree to be an outcross.

There are different uses of inbreeding, linebreeding, and outcrossing. Inbreeding is a valuable tool for targeting a particular trait, fixing it in a strain, and, as we have mentioned before, culling out faults. I personally see no purpose in linebreeding. Some people utilize it because they feel that they are avoiding decrease in size, infertility, and the faults that are brought to the surface by inbreeding. It is true that individuals decrease the chances of these "evils" somewhat with linebreeding, but they also correspondingly decrease the valuable aspects of inbreeding. Perhaps linebreeding is best used when an outcross is desired and the breeder wants to avoid a "rank" outcross, so he picks an outstanding individual that has some ancestors in its pedigree common to those of his strain's. Even here, it seems to me, the

Marge Gold's seven-week-old Goldmoor's Auntie Mame, a bundle of fun!

efficacy of the practice is on "shaky" ground. And outbreeding is the price we pay for not having been sufficiently selective with our brood stock in our own line. Perhaps our dogs have decreased in fertility or size and, thus, an outcross becomes essential. In my opinion, the best reason for an outcross is when an absolutely outstanding Rottweiler comes along and you want his blood in your line of dogs. I mean outstanding in every way: show points, temperament, intelligence, and every other desirable trait you can think of. One of those once-in-a-lifetime dogs. Even so, you will want to study the first three generations of the dog's pedigree carefully to determine the quality of his ancestors before you "pollute" your strain with the genetic material of an alien dog (in respect to your strain).

BREEDING BETTER ROTTWEILERS

Whatever method of breeding you decide to utilize, the most important determiner of the success of your program will be your judgment, your analysis of dogs and pedigrees, and your uncompromising selectivity in the individuals you select for brood stock. It is only natural for most breeders to select in terms of show points, for the breeding of winning show dogs is what brings the breeder the most glory. However, breeders who are truly committed to the Rottweiler breed will constantly assess and analyze the state of the breed and determine in which area improvements need to be made. Are there spots in which the breed needs shoring up? Is temperament less than ideal in many individuals? As an example, I can think of two main areas for breeders to concentrate on: longevity and soundness of hips. Longevity is a problem with all the giant breeds, and it is interesting that this is a problem at all. For, generally speaking, the larger the animal, the greater its longevity. For example, taking mammals only, small animals, such as mice, live for little over a year or two, but large animals, such as elephants and whales, live well past thirty years. (Biologists are still studying why humans are so long-lived for our size—although we are in the "large-animal" category!) However, within the species, it is the smaller individuals who normally have the greater longevity. It is thought, for example, that one reason women live longer than men may be because, generally speaking, they're smaller than men. Along that line, some of the smaller breeds of dogs, such as Toy Fox Terriers, Manchester Terriers, and Miniature Pinschers, have incredible longevity. As we go up the scale in size, longevity tends to decrease. Thus, it is not surprising to find that the Rottweiler's lifespan, while better than most large breeds, is not particularly impressive. What can breeders do about this? Well, for one thing, they should include longevity in the characteristics for which they are selecting. Of course, it is difficult to breed to old dogs, as they tend to become infertile. Besides, there is some evidence that the germ plasm from older animals may not be as good as that from younger ones. What the breeder *can* do is make longevity of the individuals in a pedigree an important part of his pedigree analysis and give that trait an important priority in his selection of brood stock.

Hip dysplasia is another problem that is particularly acute with the larger breeds, generally speaking, and it is an area that needs special attention with the Rottweiler. Now some people have muddied the waters by claiming that this disease stems basically from improper nutrition, and there *are* studies that would seem to indicate that nutrition, very scientifically applied, can circumvent the development of this disease of the femur and hip socket. However, I'm sure that even the nutritionists who have done these studies will admit that there is at least a genetic predisposition for the development of the disease. One of the discouraging things about this problem is that it is entirely possible to end up with dysplastic offspring from parents that have been OFA-certified to be free of the disease. The point here is that the genetic basis for it is probably polygenic; that is, many genes are involved in its development. For that reason, and the fact that there are likely many recessive genes involved, too, it will predictably take many generations to wipe a strain clean of the problem. Nonetheless, serious breeders will make very earnest efforts along this line.

Besides the two problems just discussed as being areas of specific concentration in breeding selections, the dedicated breeder will keep in his or her mind the qualities that are the essence of the breed, those which have brought the Rott to such public acclaim. Naturally, appearance is part of this; however, intelligence, tractability, toughness under pressure, and an in-born nature to protect people and property are every bit as important.

REPRODUCTION IN DOGS

Assuming that you are bound and determined to become a breeder of fine dogs in spite of my efforts to discourage such undertakings, it might be of interest for you to know the actual mechanics of what is involved in the breeding and raising of purebred dogs. Much of what follows is common knowledge among experienced dog people; yet, I am often amazed at how

Chow time for these seven vom Hochfeld puppies bred by Vivian Peters.

many experienced dog people there are who do *not* know these rudimentary facts.

It is commonly known that a female dog, or (more technically correct) bitch, cannot be bred until she comes into her heat cycle or period of estrus. The mechanics of dog reproduction and copulation are considerably different (as are those of many other mammals) from humans, and the heat periods and seeming lack of menstruation is one of the things that strikes most humans as markedly different. But technically bitches *do* have a menstruation, and it is the first part of the heat cycle. It consists of a reddish discharge accompanied by a swelling of the vulva. Biologists even refer to the very first sign of menstruation in bitches as the "menarche" (just as they do in humans). Menstruation in bitches serves as a cleansing of the uterus in preparation for its receiving the fertilized eggs. The menarche varies in bitches, usually occurring between eight and ten months of age; however, it can occur as early as six months (very rarely) or as late as a year-and-a-half. Thereafter, most bitches

At eight weeks, this vom Hochfeld "B" litter is full weaned and ready to go to the veterinarian for their first immunizations. Breeder: Vivian Peters.

come into heat about every six months. It is interesting to note that the dog's ancestor, the wolf, has one heat cycle a year, and some canine bitches seemingly revert to that, for some only have one cycle a year. Others are irregular, even without any pathological condition being present. Studies have been done which indicate that the duration of lighting, the health of the bitch, and the diet that she receives can all affect the timing of a bitch's heat cycles. After the red discharge stops, the bitch is ready to be bred, and normally she will begin to show an interest in mating.

The male (or dog) is different, too, in that his penis actually contains a bone in the interior part and behind it is a bulge, called the *copus cavernosum,* which is grasped by the bitch's vaginal sphincter, the *sphincter cunni.* Because of certain structures a dog lacks, prolonged copulation is necessary to insure fertilization. This is not unusual among animals, as many invertebrates, reptiles, and other mammals have some sort of locking mechanism for the transfer of spermatazoa. People new to the breeding of dogs are often surprised that the dogs "hang up" immediately

Selective breeding of any kind requires commitment to preserve the integrity of the breed, so this is why the decision to bring a litter of cute Rottweiler pups into the world should be considered very carefully. This adorable five-week-old pup, Pomac's Lexa P. Van Lare, was bred by Patrick and Olga McDonald and is owned by Greg and Lori Benkiser.

upon full penetration of the penis. However, copulation is not really over, as during the "tie" the transfer of semen is taking place, and both animals will normally stand quietly rear-to-rear during this time. Many owners prefer to hold the dogs' heads during this time to minimize movement and the possible risk of injury. Many breeders are delighted with a long tie, feeling that is a sign of an exceptionally potent stud and that the resultant litter will therefore be a large one. Experience and some studies have indicated, however, that there seems to be little relationship between the length of the tie and the size of the litter. No tie at all, however, is not a good sign, as very rarely do litters result from such matings—even though some breeders attempt to hold the animals together for the normally allotted time. To be certain of a litter, many breeders breed their animals at least twice during the bitch's heat, usually leaving two days between the matings. Other breeders are sufficiently confident (or fatalistic!) that they only breed the bitch once.

It should be needless to point out that it is absolutely necessary to keep the bitch confined to a kennel or other secure area during her heat period, as bitches are known for their lack of discrimination toward all male dogs during this time. In fact, it was probably proud and destructive mankind's foolishly anthropomorphic view of this period of a bitch's life, and her blatant "promiscuity" during this time, that gave her such a bad name in our history and our language.

CARING FOR THE BITCH IN SEASON
Should you decide to breed your female, you should not attempt this until at least her second or third heat. The bitch is still growing at the time of the first heat, and she is not physically prepared for the rigors of raising a litter. To prevent an unspayed female from mating during her heat period, you will need to take some precautions.

Never leave her unattended outside, even if tied, as males will go to great lengths to get to her. This is especially important in the middle of her cycle when she will accept and encourage a mating. To prevent the local males from discovering that she is in heat, you should take her away from her immediate surroundings to relieve herself, as the urine of a bitch in heat gives off a scent that is particularly attractive to male dogs. It is best to take her out in the car to a park or public spot, being very careful, always, to contain her on a leash and clean up all solid wastes. This may sound like a lot of trouble, but it may keep the male dogs from congregating around your house in the hopes of getting to your bitch.

Many people feel it is easier to board the female in heat at a local kennel until the season is over, but this is by far the most expensive alternative. If you should choose such an option, be sure to make it clear that the female is in heat and must be kept separated from all males.

Your veterinarian can supply you with pills that will reduce the odor of the urine during the heat period. There are also other items on the market to prevent the bloody discharge from staining household items or clothes, although most females in heat are very meticulous and tend to keep their genitals very clean.

Spaying is the permanent alternative for preventing a mating and should be considered if other preventive methods seem troublesome.

THE MATING

Once you have decided that you want to raise a litter of puppies and have selected suitable mates, you should prepare the dogs for the mating. First and foremost, both dogs—but especially the bitch—must be in very good physical condition. They should be checked for worms and other diseases before the breeding, as these can be passed on to the puppies by the bitch. The animal must be free of disease before she is allowed to beget a litter of pups.

Even though the two dogs will know instinctively how to mate, the breeder should still be present to monitor the proceedings. Once the male has penetrated the female, pressure on the penis causes a reflex action that fills a bulbous enlargement at the base of the penis. This bulb swells to five times its normal size within the female, locking the two animals together. This is called the "tie" and the animals usually remain tied together for fifteen to thirty minutes after the male ejaculates. The breeder must supervise to prevent a sudden attempt by either dog to pull away, as this could result in serious injury—both physical and emotional—to either the stud or bitch.

THE STUD FEE

Prior to the mating, settle *in writing* the terms of the stud service. The owner of the stud usually charges a fee, but he or she may instead prefer to take a puppy from the resultant litter. This may be the "pick of the litter" (first selection) or a second or third choice, which allows the owner of the bitch to make the first selection. While the payment of a stud fee does not in itself guarantee a litter, it does generally confer the right to breed the bitch and stud again at her next season in the event no puppies be born from the first mating.

The agreement should be precisely stated, including such details as at what age the selection of puppies should be made and what happens if only one puppy is produced from the mating.

PREGNANCY

The average gestation period for dogs is sixty-three days, although this may vary a week in either direction. Bitches expecting large litters often whelp a little early, while a small litter may go a few days overdue.

Signs of pregnancy are hard to detect, although many bitches tend to lose their appetite or vomit a week or so after the mating, indicating an upset stomach due to hormone change. Aside from this, there will be no real noticeable physical changes in the bitch until the fourth or fifth week. At this time the bitch will begin to show an expanding abdomen and enlarged nipples with a color change. A clear discharge will usually appear around the fifth week and continue through the birth of the puppies. This should be washed off, at least once a day, with a mild soap and warm water solution.

Throughout the pregnancy you should supplement the bitch's meals with vitamins and minerals to help her maintain her strength and to whelp more easily. Your veterinarian can prescribe the appropriate dosages.

The puppies grow considerably in the last three weeks before birth, so the mother must be made to eat a sufficient, well-balanced diet during this high-growth period. At this time she will have little spare room in the abdomen and may require smaller portions given at more frequent intervals. If she should refuse her food, tempt her with her favorite treats or with pieces of chicken or liver to stimulate the appetite.

While exercise is important throughout the pregnancy, strenuous exercise should be avoided as she nears the final weeks. Take her for leisurely walks at least twice a day to help her maintain muscle tone and to keep up her strength. Discourage her from doing any jumping or from climbing a lot of stairs, which could induce early labor.

PREPARING FOR THE PUPPIES

Approximately a week before the puppies are due, you should prepare a whelping box and the area to which the mother and pups will be confined. Choose a location that is warm, well lit, and fairly quiet. For ease and cleanliness, it is best if the area is close to a source of water. Allow the bitch to investigate and become accustomed to this birthing area and encourage her to sleep there prior to the actual birth.

A whelping box is needed for the birth of the litter and for the first few weeks of their life. Introduce the bitch to her box before the birth so that she will feel comfortable with it and will therefore use it (rather than making a nest in your bed or in some other inappropriate spot). Whether you purchase a whelping box or construct your own, keep in mind that it should not be too big. It should be large enough to allow the bitch to lay comfortably but not so large that she cannot reach the sides when stretching out. During labor most bitches like to push against the sides of the whelping box with their legs to aid in the delivery of the puppies. After the birth, a fairly snug box will aid

The vom Hochfeld "E" litter enjoys one of its first meals. Breeder: Vivian Peters.

in keeping the pups warm and near the dam, rather than letting them move away from the security of their mother.

The size of the box will depend on the size of the bitch. The sides should be at least high enough to keep the puppies inside, while at the same time low enough to allow the mother to get out after she has nursed her brood. The sides also prevents drafts from chilling the puppies. In cold weather, it is advisable to raise the box an inch or so off the floor to further protect against drafts.

Inside the box you should construct a guard rail two or three inches from the bottom to allow the puppies space to crawl. This will prevent the mother from rolling over on them and possibly smothering them accidentally. This rail should be made of wood and should extend out far enough so as to keep the bitch from pressing against the sides of the box.

The base of the whelping box should be covered with several layers of newspapers. These paper layers will absorb any fluids expelled during the whelping and they can be easily changed. Some breeders line the bottom of the box with carpeting to make it more comfortable and then place the newspapers on top. Once the puppies are a few days old, remove the newspapers and insert a soft towel or blanket instead. This new surface will offer the puppies more traction as they begin to climb around, and it will be more comfortable for all. The bedding should be removed daily and laundered. Be sure to secure any large piece of bedding to protect the puppies from getting tangled in it or from possibly suffocating in the loose material.

WHELPING SUPPLIES

Prior to the birth, set up a tray or table with all the supplies you will need during the whelping. You should have these items close at hand: a few small terry cloth towels or washcloths, soap, iodine, a small pair of blunt-tipped scissors, alcohol (to keep the scissors sterile), a thermometer, sterile gauze pads, white thread, a waste container, a small box lined with towels for the puppies, and a heating pad or hot water bottle to keep the puppy box warm. A scale for weighing each puppy at birth is also recommended.

The small box for the puppies is used between births. Be sure that it is adequately lined with soft, absorbent material and that it is kept warm. When placing the puppies in the box, be sure they are dry. The puppies are temporarily removed from the whelping box because their dam may become preoccupied with the next birth and, therefore, may accidentally injure the newborns. The removal should be done carefully so as not to upset the dam, and the box containing the puppies should be kept within her sight.

If possible, raise the temperature in the whelping room to 80°F. Keep a room thermometer near the whelping box to monitor the temperature in the puppies' environment. It is recommended that the whelping box be maintained at 85°F for the first two weeks.

WHELPING

As the time for whelping nears, try to spend as much time as possible with the bitch to comfort her. She may exhibit some early signs that labor is imminent, such as digging, tearing newspaper, and generally acting restless. A drop in temperature to approximately 99°F is a true indication that whelping will begin in the next twelve to twenty-four hours. You should begin monitoring the bitch's temperament several days before she is due to be aware of any change in pattern. Should her temperature fall below 99°F and remain constant for more than twenty-four hours without any signs of labor, contact your veterinarian, as she may be in need of medical attention. Alternatively, should her temperature rise to more than 102°F, you should consult your veterinarian, as an infection may be present.

The birth process will take place in three stages: (1) the early labor and dilation of the uterine passages, (2) the contractions and eventual expulsion of the whelp, and (3) the expulsion of the afterbirth (one for each puppy).

Remain with the bitch throughout the birth, but interfere only when absolutely necessary. Should the bitch appear to be having severe contractions for more than an hour without producing a whelp, veterinary attention should be sought before the dog reaches the point of exhaustion, which endangers the lives of both the whelps and the bitch.

The whelp generally will be presented head first, but feet first presentation (breech birth) is also common. Once the whelp begins to emerge, it should take only a few more contractions and pushes from the dam to eject it. Let the dam do the work. If she seems to abandon the pup or fail to remove the membrane covering the puppy's head, you must then take over and tear it open. Once the puppy is delivered, the mother will lick her newborn to dry and stimulate it. Should she fail in this, place the whelp in a clean, rough towel. Rub the pup briskly, holding it

Facing page Ch. Inner Sanctums Oh Jezebel, C.D., pictured at two years. Owned by Greg and Lori Benkiser of Van Lare Rottweilers, she is by Am. and Can. Ch. Graudstark's Pegasus, C.D. ex Inner Sanctums Phoebe.

with its head pointed downward to help drain any fluids that may be present in the lungs. Then gently clean out the pup's mouth with a gauze pad or cotton swab to remove all mucus.

The placenta (afterbirth) is usually expelled immediately after the whelp, but it may be retained for up to ten minutes. Make sure it is expelled, as a retained afterbirth can cause serious infection. Once the placenta has been passed, the mother will bite and sever the umbilical cord; she may then eat the afterbirth. The afterbirth, incidentally, contains a generous supply of vitamins and minerals, as well as a hormone that aids in uterine contraction and stimulates milk production. Allow the dam to eat one or two of these. Remove all others, however, as the afterbirth also contains a laxative that can be detrimental in large amounts.

If the umbilical cord is wrapped around the whelp's neck or if the dam fails to bite the cord, you must rectify these situations. If the latter occurs, hold the afterbirth above the whelp; allow any fluid in the umbilical cord to drain to the puppy, as it is rich in nutrients. Using a piece of cotton thread, tie a knot about one inch from the whelp's body. Use the blunt-tipped scissors and cut directly above the knot. Apply a few drops of iodine to the umbilical stub to help disinfect it, and then return the puppy to its mother.

The whelps should be encouraged to begin nursing immediately after birth. If they do not naturally find their way to a teat, place them there and stroke them to encourage their nursing instincts. The pups should be taken away only when the birth of another whelp is imminent, and they should be placed in the warm puppy box until the birth is complete. The nursing of the pups will encourage the dam's milk production. Supplementation with puppy formula should not be attempted for at least several days, unless a problem arises with the dam's milk supply.

The birth of each whelp should occur at regular intervals, but the pattern will vary with each dam and each whelping—from five minutes to several hours apart. Once you believe all the pups have been whelped, have the dam examined by your veterinarian to make sure she is in good condition and that all pups and afterbirths have been expelled. The veterinarian will most likely give her an injection of calcium and vitamin D, which helps prevent eclampsia, and a dose of hormone to help clean out the uterus.

The veterinarian usually will give the puppies a quick examination for general condition. If all is in order, leave the dam and pups alone for several hours to rest and regain their strength. Return in several hours and encourage the dam to leave the whelping box to relieve herself. You should then clean up the box and attend to the dam, since she might need a quick wash. While she is out of her box, give her a drink of water and a small offering of food.

Try to establish a daily, and later a weekly, pattern of checking on the growth of the puppies. Weigh each one shortly after birth and then again two days later. There should be a slight weight increase. If no gain is seen in several days, consult your veterinarian. As each pup matures, observe its overall health and growth patterns (the bite, eyes, testicles, legs, etc.). Be sure to clip the puppies's nails as soon as they begin to grow; otherwise the pups may scratch and irritate their dam as they nurse.

CAESAREAN SECTION

Caesarean sections are usually resorted to after the dam has been in hard labor for several hours without producing a whelp. It is essential that dogs not be allowed to labor too long, until they reach a point of exhaustion, as this tremendously increases their chances of going into shock and not surviving the operation. The fruitless labor is often the result of a pelvis that is too shallow to allow passage of the whelp, an unusual presentation of the whelp, or a toxic or life-threatening condition for either the dam or her whelps.

A Caesarean section involves cutting through the walls of the

Overleaf captions 1. Greg and Lori Benkiser's Pomac's Lexa P. Van Lare by Ch. Radio Ranch's Axel v. Notara ex Ch. Hallmark's "The Sting" at six weeks. 2. Lexa during show training at seven months. 3. Eleven-month-old Ch. Pomac's Graf Tanzer by Am. and Can. Ch. Graudstark's Pegasus, C.D. Like Lexa, "Tan" was out of Ch. Hallmark's "The Sting" and is owned by Greg and Lori Benkiser. 4. Graf Tanzer at two years.

1

3

2

4

dam's abdomen and uterus to remove the puppies. In recent years there have been great advances in the types of anesthetics used and the methods for administering them, making the risk to the dam minimal—provided she is not in an overly exhausted condition. During a Caesarean birth, the puppies are affected by the anesthetic given to the dam and they are often slow to begin breathing once removed from the womb. Should this occur, artificial respiration, as well as brisk rubbing, will induce breathing. It is imperative that the puppies be kept warm after birth, and it is advisable to place a heating pad set on low or a hot water bottle in the whelping box with the mother and whelps to provide a little extra warmth. The puppies should not, however, be allowed to return to the mother until she is alert and free of the effects of the anesthetic.

Despite a discomfort in the now-stitched abdominal region, the new mother will want her pups near her and nursing to begin. While the milk flow may be temporarily delayed after a Caesarean section, the suckling of the puppies will quickly stimulate milk production. The mother should be closely monitored for the next few days—her temperature taken twice daily—to make sure an infection does not occur. Should her temperature rise to over 102°F, a veterinarian should be consulted immediately. The stitches should be examined daily for signs of inflammation and she should be kept very clean during the healing process. The bedding should be removed and laundered daily.

POSTPARTUM CARE

The dam will insist on remaining close to her whelps for the first week, generally leaving only to relieve herself. As the pups grow in strength, she may leave for more extended periods. During this time she will not want interruptions from strangers, so try to keep her as isolated as possible.

Keep a fresh supply of water available at all times. She will want little of this in the first twenty-four hours, but broth is

Overleaf caption   Ch. Pomac's Graf Tanzer, owned by Greg and Lori Benkiser of Van Lare Rottweilers, goes Reserve Winners Dog to his brother at Westminster, 1983.

usually an enticement she won't refuse. Offer her milk several times a day, since she needs as much fluid intake as possible to help with her own milk supply. She can be given small portions of solid food after the first day, such as ground beef or chicken. She will soon need little tempting to eat, as she will have a ravenous appetite to make up for the calories expended during nursing. She will need two large meals a day, and a supply of dry food should be made available to her at all times. Her diet should be high in protein and calcium.

ECLAMPSIA

Eclampsia, or "milk fever," is a convulsive condition that is caused by a low calcium content in the bitch's blood. It can occur in late pregnancy or during the nursing period, and it is a life-threatening condition.

Symptoms are nervousness, a stiffening of the legs, pale gums, and excessive panting. Onset of the disease is often not obvious. Upon noticing a temperature increase to 102°F, veterinary attention should be sought immediately. An onset of eclampsia will require an injection of calcium and vitamin D, which enables the body to utilize and absorb the calcium.

If eclampsia is suspected, the puppies must be removed from the dam to prevent a further loss of calcium due to nursing.

Overleaf captions 1. C I'm Aten vom Hochfeld, an eight-month-old male, pictured with one of his owners, Terry Gaskins. This handsome dog is also owned by Nanette Gaskins and Stephen Kennedy. Breeder: Vivian Peters. 2. A young hopeful, Alastar's I'm Mr. M vom Hochfeld, a male owned by Vivian Peters and bred by Carole Anderson. He is shown with Terry Gaskins. 3. "D" litter vom Hochfeld male pups bred by Vivian Peters. 4. Taking Winners Dog at the 1983 Westminster Kennel Club show is Ch. Pomac's Yoda of Dagobah, owned by Patrick and Olga McDonald. His litter brother, Ch. Pomac's Graf Tanzer, takes Reserve Winners Dog. Graf Tanzer is owned by Greg and Lori Benkiser. 5. Am. and Can. Ch. Donnaj Green Mtn Boy, handled by Ross Pettruso for his owner Tony Attalla, was bred by Jan Marshall of Donnaj Rottweilers. 6. Ch. Donnaj Herr I Am, C.D., TT, owned by Jan Marshall and Bob Hogan, is by Am. and Can. Ch. Donnaj Vt Yankee of Paulus, C.D.X., TT ex Lady's Fraulein von Kristian. 7. Going Best of Winners at the Genesee County Kennel Club show is Ch. Radio Ranch's Ten of Goldmoor by Ch. Radio Ranch's Axel v. Notara (an all-time top producer) ex Ch. Susan von Anderson. Breeder: Pamela C. Brown. Owner: Marge R. Gold. 8. Ch. Radio Ranch Ebony Gold Bar, by Am. and Can. Ch. Astro v. Chisstenbrad ex Radio Ranch's Gypsy v. Notara, was a winner of the *Dog World* Award of Canine Distinction. Bred by Vina Beschard and owned by Marge R. Gold.

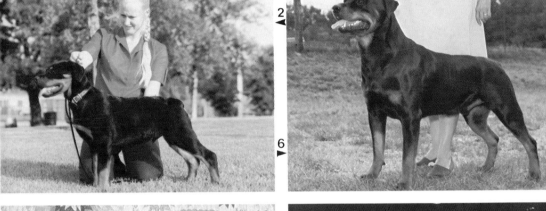

Ludwig

MASTITIS

This condition is an inflammation of the mammary glands, caused by an excess of milk. As milk accumulates, the gland becomes congested and painful for the dam. It occurs because the gland is not being thoroughly drained, often due to weak suckling or due to small litters that are unable to attend to all the tests equally.

If left uncorrected, mastitis can lead to a bacterial infection which requires antibiotics. Once the condition is indicated, treat the inflamed teat either by placing a pup on it to more fully empty it or by gently hand-expressing the milk. By careful rotation of the puppies, mastitis can be quickly cleared up.

RECORDKEEPING

During the birth process have a notebook handy to record important information regarding the whelping. Take care to monitor the vital signs of the bitch and make note of any unusual patterns or problems that may arise. This data may be helpful later on (for your veterinarian) should the bitch develop any complications.

Document the birth of each pup and the expulsion of its afterbirth. Later, transfer your notes onto a separate card for each puppy and maintain a master register of all your information. This will prove valuable whenever you need to evaluate a particular litter or your overall breeding plan. You may also want to pass on all pertinent information to the new owners of the puppies that you sell.

The following details should be recorded for each litter:

- name of the dam and sire
- date of mating
- approximate due date
- actual whelping date
- length of whelping (for each puppy)
- problems of the dam in whelping

Overleaf caption Nice head study of C I'm Aten vom Hochfeld. Bred by Vivian Peters, he is owned by Nanette and Terry Gaskins and Stephen Kennedy.

- number of puppies in litter
- sex ratio of puppies
- defects or deaths in the litter
- evaluation of the puppies (made at several weeks of age)

The following details should be recorded for each puppy:

- birth weight
- problems at birth
- date of birth
- litter registration number
- registration numbers of dam and sire
- identifying marks
- date sold
- price
- conditions of sale
- name, address, and telephone number of new owner
- name of dog (if given)

You may be one of those people who finds ample reward in spite of all the trials and tribulations of breeding dogs and raising puppies. If so, good for you! However, if, at the end of an exhausting day, you have to tend to sick pups or even just change the papers in the whelping box and you find yourself, in your darkest moment, wondering if *anything* could possibly be worth so much time and trouble, don't forget that I warned you!

Overleaf caption 1. Ch. Shearwater Jubilee Aja, TT, owner-handled to her Best of Breed over special males by Anna Marie Confessore (later Reilly). Co-owned with James Reilly, she is by Ch. Tobar's Colonel Crunch ex Shearwater Misty Morn. 2. Ch. Donnaj Happy Hooker, a full sister to Ch. Donnaj Green Mtn Boy, is pictured owner-handled by Bob Hogan. Happy Hooker is also owned by Jan Marshall. 3. Von Staten Black Diamond by Am. and Vnz. Ch. Graudstark's Kona, C.D. ex Ch. Graudstark's Rhapsody. Black Diamond finished his C.D. at fourteen months and is owned by Virginia Koerber and Anita Warner. 4. Ch. Radio Ranch's Bad Girl, handled by Darrell Hayes for owner Arthur Coia of Southwind Farms. Bad Girl was sired by Radio Ranch's Axel v. Notara out of Ch. Susan von Anderson.

1

3

BEST OF
BREED

SUFFOLK COUNTY
KENNEL CLUB INC

QUALIFYING
OBEDIENCE
ROCKLAND COUNTY
KENNEL CLUB
1983

ASHBEY

2

BEST OF
OPPOSITE
NORTH SHORE
KENNEL CLUB
1982

ASHBEY

BEST OF
WINNERS
GREATER LOWELL
KENNEL CLUB
1984

ASHBEY

4

1▲ 2▼

Chapter 7

Puppy Care

Before your puppy is able to take his place in your home, he will have gone through many formative stages that help shape his later character traits and habits. The following transitional stages mark his early growth.

From birth to two weeks of age the puppy's needs are simple: warmth, food from his dam, and lots of sleep. The ears begin to function at around ten days and the eyes open at ten to fourteen days. During this stage people should talk softly and stroke the puppy but avoid trying to pick him up or separate him from his mother.

At three to four weeks of age the puppy takes his first steps and begins to interact with his littermates. He begins to vocalize and investigate his immediate surroundings. During this stage, the puppy can be held and exposed to the noises of the household. His first supplementary food can be introduced into the diet, thereby beginning the weaning process.

At five to seven weeks of age the puppy is getting his first lessons in self-control. Weaning continues and the mother begins teaching him discipline and manners. The puppy is star-

Overleaf captions Two generations represented here. 1. Von Staten Danke Schon by Am. and Vnz. Ch. Graudstark's Kona, C.D. 2. Danke Schon's dam, Ch. Graudstark's Rhapsody. Both mother and daughter are owned by Virginia Koerber.

ting to enjoy actively socializing with his littermates and with humans. This is a vital stage in the puppy's character development, as exposure to various people and situations prepares him for his eventual place in domestic life. Puppies removed from the litter at this point often make poor pets, as they cannot adequately relate to other dogs or humans; they are either too nervous or overly aggressive. At this stage the puppy learns how to get around, taking on such challenges as stairs and thick carpets inside the house or tall grass and paved walkways outside.

From eight to ten weeks of age the puppy is fully weaned from his mother. He needs exposure to plenty of new locations and stimuli at this point, and the more positive human contact he can receive, the better. The puppy learns to want the company of people, not just of his mother and littermates. Simple training, such as teaching him his name or how to walk on a leash, can begin at this time. The puppy also should be allowed to explore his surroundings. Training at this age should be fun, not formal and not stressed. Inquisitive, active puppies can get themselves into dangerous situations, so the puppy must be supervised at this age. If not, he may chew electric cords or injure himself in rambunctious play.

At eleven to twelve weeks of age the puppy is well socialized and ready for his new home. While separation from his littermates will be traumatic, the excitement of a new life will quickly entice him and win him over. At this point the puppy goes on to develop his own personality, and simple obedience and housebreaking training can begin.

Overleaf captions   1. This wonderful series, which depicts the Rottweiler in protection-dog training, was submitted to us by Kent Freeman. 1. Greg with Centurion Mr. Stubbs, better known as "Barney." 2. On a warm day, this agitator (Larry Katz) sheds the upper-body padding in hopes that he can use his skill and the sleeve to keep the dog off him. 3. Since Barney is not completely trained yet as a protection dog, he is worked on lead as a precautionary measure for the agitator. 4. The agitator has "surrendered," and the dog has been put on "watch" command. The dog will attack only if the agitator moves. 5. Barney is on a "sit-watch" command. 6. Here he is on a "down-watch" command. 7. The agitator makes an aggressive move toward the protection dog's owner, and the dog immediately goes into action. 8. This is light agitation, with the agitator never coming any closer to the dog's owner than he is now.

1 ►

5 ►

2 ►

6 ►

3 ►

7 ►

4 ►

8 ►

SELECTING YOUR PUPPY

Before you begin the search for that special puppy to share your home, there are several issues that you must first resolve. The most important question of all is whether or not you are ready to commit yourself to being a responsible dog owner. Is there time in your life to devote to your new companion, or will he be left alone for long stretches of time while you are at work or school? Are *all* members of your family happy about getting a puppy or do some view him as an intrusion? Questions such as these must be honestly answered before you make the decision to get a puppy, as this is a long-term commitment and you must do what is best for both you and the animal.

MALE OR FEMALE?

While dogs of both sexes make good pets, there are a few differences that you may want.to consider. If you are interested in breeding and raising a litter of puppies, you should, of course, select a good-quality female (a bitch). Those who do not plan on breeding their dogs should bear in mind that a nonneutered female will attract males whenever she comes into heat. These heat cycles occur approximately every six months, last two to three weeks, and can be very annoying. Spaying will eliminate this problem. Females are generally regarded as a little more gentle than males, and, therefore, have been acclaimed as better housepets.

Males are often slightly larger than their female counterparts, with a higher activity level and a stronger tendency to roam.

Overleaf captions   A continuation of the protection-dog training series submitted by Kent Freeman. 1. This Rottweiler learns to guard the car. 2. Here he learns to guard the fences of his owner's property. 3. Muzzle work is important to keep a dog from becoming what is known as "sleeve happy." 4. The agitator is hard pressed, even against his muzzled Rottweiler, because of the animal's tremendous strength. 5. Even though the dog has a muzzle on, the agitator has his hands full because the Rottweiler is such a large, powerful canine. 6. "Titan" responds to aggression by the agitator, and 7. he stands guard while a "suspect" is frisked. 8. Angus vom Hochfeld, known to his owner as "Grizzly," is pictured in training as a police dog for the El Cajon Police Department. Owned and worked by his owner, Officer Mike Howard, he is trained by Bert Quick. Breeder: Vivian Peters. This last photo in the protection-dog training series was submitted by Vivian Peters.

While both sexes are equally loving and loyal, females have been touted as superior watchdogs because they are less likely to be distracted by outside forces. Males, however, are noted for being more aggressive against intruders.

WHAT AGE IS BEST?

While puppies certainly are the most adorable at six weeks of age, this is not the most advantageous age from an owner's point of view. At six weeks the puppy is like a baby that requires care twenty-four hours a day. He is too young to reliably housebreak, he requires four or more feedings a day, and he is undisciplined. In fact, a much higher percentage of four- to-six-week-old puppies die shortly after being placed with new owners than do eight-week-olds who have greater stamina. From an economic standpoint, it is certainly best for breeders or pet shops to sell their puppies when they are very young; they do not incur the additional expense of those first few trips to the veterinarian. But from a buyer's standpoint, one must consider how much time one has to devote to a puppy's early care before setting out to purchase that new family member.

Purchase your puppy when you find the one you feel will be best for you—whether he is six weeks old or six months old. One possible solution for dealing with primary puppy care is to board the six-week-old puppy with the breeder for a month or two after you purchase him. Experienced breeders are generally more adept at dealing with the needs of puppies and may be amenable to this arrangement for a fee, of course. If you are considering the purchase of an adult dog that has never been kept as a housepet, be sure to check his disposition carefully, as he may have trouble adjusting to family life.

Overleaf captions 1. Ch. Lucene's Laura, C.D., bred and owned by Michelle Sudinski, sits alongside Ch. Der Catlin's H H Dieter, C.D., bred by Susan Catlin and owned by Vivian Peters. 2. Five-week-old Goldmoor's Robin Hood, bred and owned by Marge R. Gold. 3. Sir Butkus Baby Bull (known as "Titan") with owner, Sheriff Jay Sheffield. 4. Cheyenne vom Hochfeld at twelve months. Bred by Vivian Peters, owned by LaVonne Christensen. 5. Six-week-old Southwind's Dulcinea, owned by Arthur Coia of Southwind Farms. 6. A Welkerhaus portrait, also used on one of their Christmas cards! Photo courtesy of Rita Welker of Welkerhaus Rottweilers.

SHOW QUALITY OR PET QUALITY?

When purchasing your purebred puppy, you must decide whether you want him to be a companion or whether you want to show him in competition. This is very important because only the finest breed specimens should be entered into active competition. Show-quality puppies are the hardest to find and are the most expensive to buy. If you are not interested in dog-show exhibiting, any healthy, well-bred specimen of the breed should do.

If showing is your intention, you should buy a puppy from a knowledgeable and reputable breeder. The puppies available in pet shops or from most neighborhood owners are generally termed "pet quality." This does not mean that they will make inferior or superior pets as compared to show-quality dogs; it just means that they are somehow slightly faulty when measured against the breed's standard of perfection. This faultiness is rarely evident to anyone except a breeder or dog-show judge and is of great concern only when you are entering the dog in competition. Be sure to make your desire to show the dog clear to the breeder so that he or she will sell you the best specimen possible that you can afford. Dedicated breeders strive to produce the finest dogs they can, ones that will enhance the quality of the breed. Not all dogs owned by even the top breeders are of superior quality when compared against the standard; therefore, a breeder may stipulate that you may not breed the pet-quality animal and thereby pass on his faulty traits. So bear this in mind and be sure to clarify your breeding intentions at the time of sale. Also, be aware that you will pay top prices for show dogs and for those females with brood bitch potential.

ONE DOG OR MORE?

Dogs, once they mature from puppyhood, generally prefer the attention of humans to the companionship of another dog, so there is no real need to buy your puppy a companion unless he is to be left alone a lot of the time. If this is the case, the second dog

Overleaf caption Head study of the noble Ch. Der Catlin's H H Dieter, C.D., owned by Vivian Peters of vom Hochfeld and bred by Susan C. Catlin of der Catlin.

118

may help counteract loneliness, but you run the risk of having two unhappy pets on your hands.

If you are introducing a puppy into a home with an older dog, remember that there will be a period of adjustment for both dogs. The older dog may manifest signs of jealousy and resent the intrusion of the puppy. To counteract this, be sure to give the older dog lots of attention. At feeding time be sure to watch both dogs—especially the puppy, who, not knowing the rules, may try to steal from the other dog's bowl. Most adult dogs will accept a new dog in the home after a day or two; but if either dog shows any aggressiveness, you may want to keep them separated. Introduce them to each other for short periods of time until they become more accustomed to each other.

PURCHASING YOUR PUPPY

Once you've decided that you are ready to commit yourself to being a good owner and you've selected those characteristics and traits that you want in your dog, where do you go to locate that specific puppy you've been thinking so much about? You have several options.

If a pet-quality puppy is what you have in mind, start with your local newspaper and see if there are any ads for locally-bred litters. You can also obtain pet-quality puppies from established kennels who generally price their dogs according to their show potential. While you may pay more for a puppy from a professional breeder than you would from a local mating, you may be able to see several generations of your dog's ancestors at the breeder's kennel. This should give you a good indication of what your puppy will look and act like when it grows up. Make sure you see both or at least one of the puppy's parents.

In the case of a show-quality puppy, it is best if you visit more than one breeder and evaluate as many litters as you can find, even if you think you've found the right dog. You should be able to locate several breeders in your area by consulting the ads in newspapers and the various publications distributed by dog

Overleaf caption Ch. Altar's Gunner of Woodland by Ch. Radio Ranch's Axel von Notara ex Ch. Gudrun von Anderson.

clubs. If you are looking for a true top-quality specimen, you should attend some dog shows and talk to the exhibitors. Some may have puppies or young dogs for sale or know of some people who do. At the very least, these breed enthusiasts can acquaint you with the finer points of what to look for and give you inside information on how to proceed, where to go, and what to pay.

SIGNS OF GOOD HEALTH

When evaluating litters of puppies in an attempt to select the one that is right for you, what should you look for? Your primary concern should be for signs of good health. A puppy should look plump and well-fed. His ribs and hip bones should not be protruding prominently. A very thin or potbellied puppy may have worms and should be carefully inspected by a veterinarian. A healthy puppy should have clear eyes and there should be no discharge from his eyes or nose. The coat should be filling in nicely, without bare patches or obvious sores, and there should be no sign of a rash on the inside of the dog's legs or on his abdomen. Check his hearing ability by standing behind the puppy and making loud noises. He should quickly respond to the commotion and turn to you. Given that most puppies you see will pass this basic health exam, what else should you be looking for?

Among a litter of healthy puppies, one may stand out as the most jovial or outgoing. He may do things to attract your attention and generally seem to like you, as if he has picked *you* for his own! Be sure he is vigorous and of similar size with his littermates. Generally the runt or giant of the litter does not grow into the best specimen. He should be alert and full of energy, not listless and shy. A puppy's feet and bones will look out of proportion with his size. Don't worry, he will eventually balance

Overleaf captions 1. Ch. V. Gailingen's Welkerhaus Cia, by Ch. Igor von Schauer ex Ch. Anka von Gailingen, pictured winning Best of Opposite Sex at sixteen months. Rita Welker, owner. 2. Virginia Koerber's Ch. Graudstark's Kona, C.D., the 1977 specialty Winners Dog, Colonial Rottweiler Club. 3. Eleven-month-old La Ranch's Polo Bear B, TT, owner-breeder-handled by Anna Marie Reilly to Reserve Winners Dog from the puppy classes under noted judge Roxanne Mahan. Polo Bear is co-owned with James Reilly. 4. Sidney Lamont handles Graudstark's Andromeda at a Windham County Kennel Club show in 1982 for owner Virginia Koerber.

out. Concern yourself with his general appearance and that of the area he has been raised in. A caring, thoughtful breeder will not allow his breeding quarters and animals to become infested with parasites, and such good breeding care often results in healthy, lively dogs.

Once you have selected your puppy, arrange with the owner to allow the dog to be taken to your veterinarian for a health examination. Most breeders or pet shops will let you return the dog within a few days if he should fail the health exam for any reason. Get this in writing, and be sure of the terms. Some owners will replace the ailing dog with another dog and some will return all your money. This agreement, however, generally does not apply if you have a change of heart; it applies only if the dog is certified, by the vet, as being physically unfit.

Before you take the puppy home, be sure to ask the breeder for all of the puppy's inoculation and health records. The breeder also may be able to familiarize you with some of your puppy's habits or personality traits. Did he have a favorite toy or blanket that you could take home with you to help ease the transition to his new home? Ask what and how often the puppy has been fed. Try not to vary this diet very much once you have gotten him home, to avoid possible stomach or bowel upset. Some thoughtful breeders often give the new owners a few days' supply of the puppy's food so that he can continue eating the same food in his new environment.

PAPERS

At the time of sale, arrange with the breeder to furnish you with your purebred puppy's registration papers from the national kennel club. Depending on the age of the dog, you may be given the registration application or the completed registration certificate, if this has already been received back from the registering body. Once a litter is born, the breeder generally applies to register the litter, specifying the names of the sire and dam and stating the number of puppies. The governing kennel

Overleaf caption Ch. Der Catlin's H H Dieter, C.D. pictured with his friend and handler, Terry Gaskins. Bred by Susan C. Catlin and owned by Vivian Peters.

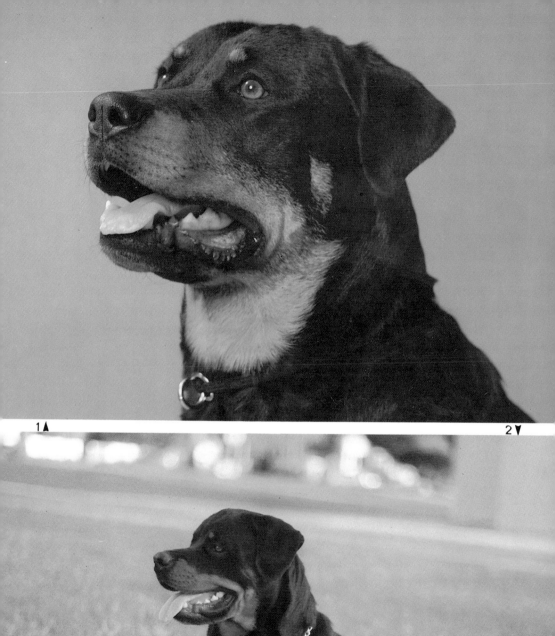

club then issues a registration application for each of the qualifying puppies. If you are purchasing a six-to-ten-week-old puppy, this application will most likely be what you receive. With this, you will give the dog his official name and transfer ownership of the puppy from the breeder to you. The breeder will have to supply some of the information on the form, so discuss this application procedure with him or her if you are not sure how to proceed.

If you are purchasing a slightly older dog, he may have been registered with the national kennel club and a registration certificate may have already been issued. In this case you will need to write to the national club to arrange a transfer of ownership. If transfer forms are not available from the breeder, such forms can be obtained by writing to:

The American Kennel Club
51 Madison Avenue
New York, New York, 10010

The Kennel Club of Great Britain
1 Charges Street
Piccadilly, London W1, England

The Canadian Kennel Club
111 Eglinton Avenue East
Toronto, Ontario M6S 4V7

The Australian Kennel Club
Royal Show Grounds
Ascot Vale, Victoria, Australia

Occasionally a breeder may purposely withhold the puppy's registration certificate from the new owner. This is generally done because the dog has a fault that is disqualifying, according to the breed or dog-show standards. This does not mean that the dog will not make a good pet, rather that the breeder is striving to eliminate the disqualifying traits from his dogs' future offspring. He may stipulate that the only way he will sell such a pet-quality animal is if the new owner agrees not to breed him. Once the puppy has been neutered, the breeder usually will render the registration material, should the owner still want the dog registered. Through the actions of such conscientious breeders, the overall quality of purebred dogs is enhanced for future generations.

Overleaf captions 1. Pandemonium's Jet Black Jazz by Ch. Eiko vom Schwaiger Wappen, C.D.X. ex Graudstark's Pandemonium. Linda Wagner, owner. 2. Baldrick vom Hochfeld at nine months. "Bear" was bred by Vivian Peters and is owned by Chris Hagood.

THE FIRST DAY HOME

Hopefully you have already prepared an area of your home for the new arrival and stocked up on the items you and he will need in the early weeks:

> puppy food
> food and water bowls
> brush and comb
> bed or sleeping box
> collar and leash (or a one-piece lead)

The first day in a new home is going to be traumatic for your puppy, and very young puppies can be particularly unnerved. Try to make the transition easy for him by letting him get acquainted with the new environment on his own. Continuous play and attention will quickly overtire him. While it may take a lot of willpower on your part, try to keep the attention you give him to a minimum. Show him to his quarters, supplying him with some water and a little food, and leave the rest up to him. After a little rest, the puppy may be better prepared to meet all the members of his new family. A cautious introduction such as this will not overwhelm the puppy and will make him eager, not fearful, to learn more about his new surroundings.

Be sure in the first meeting that all family members, especially children, know the proper method of handling and picking up a puppy. You should place one hand under his hindquarters and the other across the chest. Never pick him up by the paws or legs or by the back of the neck. This could damage the still immature muscles and ligaments.

While you should start housebreaking lessons the first day, don't be too stern or expect the puppy to really understand what's expected of him. Mistakes are bound to happen, so confine the puppy to a small area. Provide him with a sleeping box or a bed for his naps, and try to comfort and reassure him if he starts to cry. The puppy should be kept indoors until he has received his first round of immunizations.

THE PUPPY BED OR SLEEPING BOX

Whether you intend to let your dog sleep in the house or

whether you will eventually supply him with a dog house in the yard, it is advisable to keep him indoors until he is about six months old—especially during cold periods of the year. The puppy bed is not only an effective tool in easing his transition from the security of his mother and littermates to your home, but it will also aid in the housebreaking process. Dogs are born with a natural instinct for keeping their sleeping quarters clean; so, given a choice, they will look elsewhere for a spot to relieve themselves.

A box is best for the four-to-eight-week-old puppy. You should hold off buying a bed until he is older and closer to his adult size. When choosing a spot for the bed, always place it in a warm, dry area that is free from drafts.

The puppy's box should be only slightly larger than he is. It should allow him to stand, turn around, and lie down at full length. He should not be able to make a mess in one end and lay comfortably in another. You can make an inexpensive sleeping box from a standard cardboard box. Never use a cardboard box that has previously been used to store fresh fruits or vegetables, as it may have been sprayed with pesticides to prevent spoilage. This residue could be harmful to young puppies.

Be sure to place plenty of ventilation holes in the sides of the box and line the bottom of the box with several layers of newspaper, which is easily disposable. Unless the room the box is kept in is on the chilly side, hold off putting a blanket in the box for a week or two, as the puppy tends to push the blanket into one corner and is then uncomfortable trying to sleep on it. You should also make a lid to cover the box at night. Without the lid, the puppy will continuously try to climb out of the box. This only leads to his becoming anxious and crying.

During the first days in his new home when he is to be alone—which is a new experience for him, as he has always enjoyed the companionship of his littermates and mother—you can leave a radio playing softly nearby to help soothe him. At night, placing a loud ticking clock near the box will remind him of his

Facing page A 1972 photo of Kleinste Bettina of Fair Lane, C.D., a two-year-old bitch bred by Vivian Peters and owned by Gordon K. and Dirkje Watt.

Arinov's Abraxas, at eight weeks, explores nature! By Ch. Pomac's Always A Cinch out of Ch. Tulakes Echo, C.D. Breeders: Dan and Lisa Calkins. Owner: Robert Grunder.

mother and allow him to sleep more easily. You may also want to fill a hot water bottle with warm water, wrap it in a fluffy towel, and place this in his box as another comfort. These extraordinary measures should be necessary only for the first week or two, as the puppy will quickly adjust to his new home and routine.

The puppy *wants* to keep his bed clean, but he will be forced to relieve himself if he is not taken out at regular intervals. Expect a few accidents the first few days. The newspaper bedding should be changed daily whenever this happens. As the puppy grows, you may have to get a larger box; or he may do well with his early housebreaking lessons and then you can move him to his permanent bed.

While it is necessary for a new puppy to play with and be loved by his new family, a young puppy tires easily and needs many naps each day. Try to place him in his box for as many of these naps as possible to make him feel secure in the box. This will allow him to adjust to the box and it will help to keep him from crying at night.

130

Once the puppy settles into a housebreaking routine, it is a good time to consider buying him a permanent bed. Be sure to place the bed in an area that he likes or he may not use it. Some beds come with mattresses that contain scented materials, such as cedar. Many dogs do not like this smell and will not use the bed because of it. Other dogs just don't enjoy sleeping on a dog bed and often prefer a rug or a soft piece of furniture. Hopefully you and the dog can arrange a mutually agreeable spot for him to sleep. If he should choose a place where you do not want him, correct him each time he goes to it. He may soon lose interest in the desired location if it is unavailable to him.

Some owners prefer to supply their dog with a mat to lie on, placing it either directly on the floor or in a sleeping basket. While most dogs take readily to this, be careful to buy a mat of natural fiber. Mats that are dyed can cause an allergic reaction in some dogs, which can result in skin irritations and other disorders.

HOUSEBREAKING

No aspect of dog ownership warrants more concern among owners of puppies than housebreaking. Will my puppy learn quickly? What is the easiest, most efficient method? What is the puppy to do when I am not home to let him out?

The most important point to keep in mind is that dogs instinctively want to keep their sleeping quarters clean. This will aid greatly in the housebreaking process. However, you must remember that a puppy cannot be expected to be able to control his elimination reflexes at an early age. While he is very young, it is best to anticipate his needs. He will need to relieve himself at certain times each day: after waking, after each meal, late at night, and after any period of great excitement or vigorous exercise. Until he is reliably housebroken, make sure he is in the appropriate area at these important times. Praise him when he relieves himself in his assigned spot, even if you had to whisk him there at the very last second.

Serious housebreaking can begin at three months of age, but don't expect perfection at first. A realistic goal for a dog that is completely housebroken is six months. Until then, a few "accidents" are bound to occur.

The most efficient method of housebreaking is to train the puppy directly to the outdoors; but this requires your being available to take him out whenever the need arises, as a puppy cannot be expected to wait for any length of time. The more practical, although an untidy and prolonged method, is to first paper train the puppy and then eventually break him to going outdoors.

Assign an area several feet square near the door as the temporary spot for the newspapers. The puppy should be kept confined to this room when not under direct supervision in another area of the house. Begin the paper training the first day by making use of the first "accident" you find. Soak a piece of newspaper in the puppy's urine. Save this piece and place it on the clean newspapers to serve as a scent marker for the proper area. You should have to do this only once or twice before the puppy knows where he is permitted to relieve himself.

Be sure to thoroughly clean the site of all accidents, especially carpets. If any odor is allowed to remain, the dog will recognize the scent and return to repeat his misdeed. Rinse the area with soapy water, to which a little vinegar or ammonia has been added, to overpower the smell of urine. Remove all excess water and allow the area to dry.

Always be on the lookout in the early days for signs that your pup needs to relieve himself. He may whimper or cry, look restless, sniff the floor, or run anxiously around the room. At this point you should place him on the newspapers and praise him when he uses the area. As he becomes accustomed to this process and uses the papers reliably, reduce the size of the papers.

You will probably want to eliminate the papers as soon as it is possible for the puppy to go outside when he needs to. If he is to be left alone all day while you are at work or school, however, this will take some time, as puppies cannot be expected to have complete control of their elimination reflexes until they are grown. If this is the case, keep the puppy confined to a small

Eight-week-old puppies sired by Ch. Pomac's Always A Cinch out of Ch. Tulakes Echo, C.D. Pictured with their breeders, Dan and Lisa Calkins of Arinov's Rottweilers.

area covered with the newspapers while you are out.

It is important to prevent the puppy from becoming totally dependent on the newspapers. Some paper-trained dogs have been known to play outside for hours and scratch anxiously to get into the house to use the papers when the need arises. Encourage your dog to use the designated areas outside and soon he should adapt easily to relieving himself away from the papers. Begin outdoor housebreaking at a time of day when you know he will need to relieve himself, especially in the morning as soon as he has awakened. Take him out on his leash and walk him back and forth in a small area. Praise him when he goes. He may, however, be confused about what is expected of him. You may find it easier to place a small piece of paper on the ground. This will be necessary only once or twice, as the dog will quickly learn that it is permissible to use the area you have brought him to. Regardless of whether this area is on your property or in a public place, it is the owner's responsibility to clean up all solid wastes, not only as a courtesy to everyone but also to help prevent potential health problems. "Pooper scooper" laws are in effect in many cities and towns, and failure to clean up after your dog may result in a hefty fine.

In general, a female puppy usually requires a shorter outdoor walk to accomplish her elimination mission, while a male may opt for a longer walk with more stops. He is more concerned with marking his territory. As puppies, both sexes will squat. A male dog will begin to lift his leg when he is nearly grown.

The housebreaking process should not be too drawn out if you give the dog the proper amount of attention, encouragement, and praise. Have patience and do not rush him along. Remember: *accidents do happen.* If you catch him in the act in a forbidden area, give a forceful "No!" and show him the proper area. NEVER rub his nose in his excreta. This is a degrading action that accomplishes nothing except to make him fearful and more confused. He should never be hit (even with a rolled-up newspaper), yelled at, or chased in response to a mistake, and food should never be withheld as a punishment. Correct inappropriate behavior with firm but loving guidance and make clear what the appropriate behavior should be. Praise all accomplishments.

Remember, dogs are naturally clean and want to keep their quarters clean. If you are experiencing a problem after several months of consistent training, the use of a dog crate may help eliminate the problem. When you are not available to supervise the dog, confine him to this crate. Placing a dog in a proper dog crate is not a form of punishment. Most dogs, if introduced to the crate while young, react favorably to the crate and find it comforting—it is a spot of their own. Unless your dog is ill, he will try his best not to soil the crate. However, he will still have to be taken out of the crate at regular intervals to relieve himself. The crate is a temporary aid, not a jail. He should be given plenty of time outside of it. When you think he needs relief, show him to the proper location and praise him highly when he complies with what you expect of him. As he matures and learns to control his reflexes, you will be able to remove the crate and

Six-week-old Goldmoor puppies bred by Marge R. Gold.

leave the dog alone, as long as regularly scheduled elimination intervals are maintained. No dog can be expected to endure more than eight to ten hours without relieving himself. If you cannot be available at regular intervals, you must either resign yourself to having a perpetually paper-trained dog or postpone dog ownership until a time when you can supply more attention to the animal.

If you are lucky enough to have easy access to the outdoors, you may wish to install a small flexible door for your dog to give him instant entry to the yard. Once in the yard be sure he actually tends to his business and does not forget the purpose of his trip out. There are plenty of distractions that can entice an eager puppy. Most dogs appreciate the freedom such a swinging door affords, but owners must properly secure the area to which a dog has access by fencing in the yard or constructing a dog run.

THIS SPAY/NEUTER CONTRACT HAS BEEN ENTERED INTO ON _____ 19__
BETWEEN _____,HERINAFTER CALLED
THE SELLER, AND _____
_____, HERINAFTER CALLED BUYER;
CONCERNING _____
_____ HEREINAFTER CALLED DOG.

THE BUYER HAS OBTAINED THIS DOG AT A GREATLY REDUCED PRICE
AND IN RETURN AGREE TO THE FOLLOWING.

   1. To spay/neuter the dog as soon as possible but no
       later than one year of age. The buyer binds himself
       to take proper precautions that the dog is not
       accidentally bred or used for breeding before being
       altered.

   2. The buyer cannot sell, mortgage, give away, or
       assign the dog without previous written consent of
       the seller, untill the terms of this contract are
       fufilled. The seller must be kept appraised of the
       whereabouts of the dog at all times and the buyer
       will notify seller promptly in writing of any change
       of address or phone no while the contract is in fource.

   3. The buyer understands that this contract is not to
       be entered into lightly and that if he does not honor
       the terms of this contract he must pay to the seller
       an additional $500.00 plus any court costs or attorney
       fees incurred.

THE SELLER WILL RETAIN PEDIGREE AND AKC PAPERS UNTILL PROOF
THAT THE DOG HAS BEEN RENDERED INCAPABLE OF REPRODUCTION IS
FURNISHED BY THE BUYER. A SIGNED STATEMENT FROM A VETERINARIAN
WILL BE SATISFACTORY. AT SUCH TIME THIS CONTRACT SHALL BE
CONSIDERED TERMINATED AND THE BUYER WILL RECEIVE AKC REGIS-
TRATION PAPERS AND PEDIGREE.

_____

_____

_____

_____

SELLER Vivian A. Peters   BUYER/S _____

"vom Hochfeld"   _____

6220 Japatul Highlands Rd.   _____

 Alpine, Ca. 92001   _____

 (619) 445-9367   _____

If you breed and sell Rottweilers, every transaction should be in writing. This contract and the one on the following page are samples of the ones used at vom Hochfeld. Other breeders may have their own contracts which may be different from these.

ROTTWEILER

HEREDITARY DEFECTS:
  Hip Dysplasia
  Entropion

SERIOUS FAULTS:
  Any missing tooth
  Level bite

DISQUALIFICATIONS:
  Total absence of markings
  Any base color other than black
  Overshot bite
  Undershot bite
  Four or more missing teeth
  Long coat

PET PRICE $_____SHOW/BREEDING PRICE $_____ THIS LITTER

SIRE:_____WHELPED_____

DAM:_____SEX_____

DATE_____AMT.PAID$_____DUE$_____

THIS PUPPY IS SOLD AS A SHOW/BREEDING PROSPECT; HOWEVER,
MANY OF THE HEREDITARY DEFECTS AND DISQUALIFICATIONS AND
FAULTS MAKE THEIR APPEARANCE AS THE PUPPY MATURES. A PUPPY
WHICH DEVELOPS ANY OF THE ABOVE DEFECTS OR DISQUALIFICATIONS
SHOULD NOT BE BRED. THE BUYER AT HIS DISCRETION, MAY ELECT
NOT TO BREED IF THE SERIOUS FAULTS APPEAR. A DOG EXHIBITING
ANY OF THE DISQUALIFICATIONS CANNOT BE SHOWN.

THE SELLER WILL REFUND THE DIFFERENCE BETWEEN SHOW/BREEDING
PRICE AND PET PRICE, NAMELY$_____ , IF THE PUPPY DEVEL-
OPS ANY OF THE ABOVE NAMED DEFECTS, DISQUALIFICATIONS, OR
FAULTS; AND THE BUYER PRESENTS TO SELLER A WRITTEN STATEMENT
FROM HIS VETERANARIAN THAT THE ABOVE DESCRIBED PUPPY HAS
BEEN RENDERED INCAPABLE OF REPRODUCTION. THE SELLER RETAINS
THE RIGHT TO EXAMINE THE DOG FOR DEFECTS, DISQUALIFICATIONS
AND FAULTS; BEFORE IT IS ALTERED.

DISQUALIFICATIONS, FAULTS, AND ENTROPION SHOULD BE APPARENT
BY ONE YEAR OF AGE; THEREFORE THE REFUND FOR THEASE WILL ONLY
BE GIVEN UP TO 14 MO. OF AGE AND NOT AFTER.

DIAGNOSIS OF HIP DYSPLASIA MUST BE MADE BY THE ORTHOPEDIC
FOUNDATION FOR ANIMALS (O.F.A.) AND THE SELLER IS TO RE-
CIEVE A COPY OF THEIR FINDINGS. DIAGNOSIS MUST BE MADE
BEFORE @6 MO. OF AGE IN ORDER TO RECIEVE A REFUND.

_____
_____
_____
_____
_____

"vom Hochfeld"
Vivian A. Peters
SIGNATURE OF SELLER
DATE: _____
6220 Japatul Highlands Rd.
Alpine, Ca. 92001
(619) 445-9367

SIGNATURE OF BUYER/S
DATE:_____

137

Show training starts early for twelve-week-old Pomac's Lexa P. Van Lare, owner/handled by Lori Benkiser. A Rottweiler destined for the show ring must learn to stand calmly and quietly white being "stacked" for examination by the judge.

Chapter 8

Basic Obedience Training

Discipline is a key component of the pet/owner relationship—as vital as supplying the dog with the proper amount of love and care. Obedience training ensures a happy future for all concerned, as the dog is taught the manners he will need to participate in family life.

From an early age a dog needs to know who is in charge and what is right and wrong, or he will continually test his owner. By nature, dogs think they are the boss unless there is another more dominant force in the picture. At birth, for example, the dog's mother is the boss. You must earn your position as boss by teaching your pet that only appropriate behavior will be tolerated and that you will not accept his testing of your authority. This is not accomplished by making the dog live in fear of your wrath but by teaching him what is expected of him and being consistent and fair in the enforcement of these guidelines. Once this is settled you can look forward to owning a pet who can be relied upon to be responsible in the home and in public.

Most dogs are adept at learning and therefore thrive on it. The best way to work with this natural inclination towards learning is to begin by teaching some very simple, easily accomplished tasks and progress very slowly to more complicated skills as the dog proves he understands and remembers what he has been taught. Even if you have never trained a dog before, with a little patience and effort you should be able to teach any dog such basic commands as Sit, Stay, and Come. If you exhibit a flair for training and your dog is a good learner you may want to proceed with more advanced training skills, but at the very least he will require both a basic working knowledge of how to act in common situations and the ability to be controlled.

Some common-sense rules should apply in training your dog. First of all, if you begin training with a young puppy and find that he is very confused, he may be too young to give you the concentration that is required and you would do best to postpone the lessons for a few weeks until he is older and better prepared. A puppy should be allowed some freedom while he is young, and you should not expect true obedience at an early age. If you work him too hard when he is young, you may break his spirit and be left with a fearful or overly passive adult dog. You want to begin *formal* skills training when you think the dog really understands what you want, generally around six or eight months of age, although you should certainly try to teach him your rules of right and wrong as soon as he comes to live with you.

There are a few basic rules you should follow during every training lesson. Keep the lessons fairly short and to the point, usually ten minutes in the beginning. This will enable the dog to retain his concentration and eagerness to learn. Do not let things get too unstructured so that training seems like all fun and games. Obedience is serious business and you should make the dog aware of this. You should be firm but not scolding, and be quick to praise the dog when he has done well. You should not, of course, praise him so highly that he gets overexcited and forgets all he has learned.

Consistency is a key aspect of training. You should hold your lessons regularly, not in a hit-or-miss fashion. Use the same commands each time you work on a certain skill, not Sit one time and Sit Down the next. It is also effective if you call the dog by his name before each request, such as "Sam, Sit." You should always require a consistent response from the dog; never accept a partial completion of any command.

You must be patient and be prepared for many repetitions of the desired behavior until it is learned by your dog. There is no room for anger. When you speak to the dog, use a firm, authoritative tone of voice. Do not shout at him, no matter how frustrated you may get. Such behavior will only confuse him and make things worse. Never nag at him. When you speak to him during training, mean it and be clear as to what you expect him to do. When he responds incorrectly, correct him appropriately and repeat the exercise. Correction should be made in such a way as to inspire him to do better. With each slight improvement or correct response, reward him with petting and kind words.

During the early phases of training the dog will not understand how he is expected to respond. He will learn through making errors and receiving guidance from you. Correct lovingly, not angrily. There is a definite distinction between correction and punishment. Punishment should be reserved as a response to *willful misbehavior only.* Confusion in the dog requires patient correction, not punishment from a tired, frustrated owner. Never punish a dog if you are in doubt about his intent. Constant punishment can ruin the training process, so be sure not to ask the dog to give too much during the early lessons. If you find you cannot calmly continue to supply the dog with fair correction, stop for the day and give it another try when you are well rested and at ease. Some people have great difficulty with this, and if this is the case you may want to consider hiring an experienced trainer to take over, or perhaps another family member may have better success.

To facilitate concentration for both owner and dog, plan the lessons for a time of day when hunger and tiredness do not come into play. In the summer, train in the cool of the early morning or evening; the lessons should take place in a location that has few distractions, one that is well ventilated.

One very important rule: Always end your lessons on a

positive note. If things are going well, do not get carried away and continuously push the dog to do "just one more" exercise or repetition. Praise the dog for his good work and quit for the day. Working the dog beyond the limits of his concentration will result in confusion and will set back the training process.

If things are not going well, try to reassure the dog and have him perform some very simple task that he is already familiar with to end the lesson. Praise him and let him know you appreciate the effort he is making. The next lesson hopefully will be more successful.

If you end a lesson abruptly, on a negative note, the dog will not want to participate again. He will fear displeasing you and become more of a problem with each failure. Proceed very slowly and praise each new accomplishment, no matter how small. Moving very slowly in the initial stages of training may seem tedious to you but it will pay off in the end as your dog learns how to learn. The ultimate goal is to have the dog come to enjoy and thrive on the training process, not fear it.

At the end of every lesson let your dog do something that he enjoys, such as romp in the yard or play a game of chase with you. Ending the lessons pleasantly will keep him interested and he will associate training with pleasing you and having fun. And pleasing you, pleases him.

THE EARLY LESSONS

The first lesson to teach your dog is to recognize his name. During the time you have owned your dog you have, hopefully, been calling him by one name. A short name is easiest for the dog to learn. Even the show dog with a long string of names should be called by one simple name at home. If you use his name frequently, a puppy will quickly learn to recognize it. When he responds as you call him, reward him with praise or a tidbit.

Whether or not to use food bits as rewards for proper behavior is a matter for you to consider. In the beginning training sessions, this will encourage the dog to respond to your commands, but the aim of training is to teach the dog proper behavior—not

142

Ch. Pomac's Always A Cinch (above and below), sired by Ch. Bulli von Meyerhoff out of Ch. Hallmark's "The Sting." "Rocky" is a multi-Best of Breed winner and Group placer. Owned by Dan and Lisa Calkins, Arinov's Rottweilers.

how to respond in order to receive a reward. It is best to keep such rewards infrequent and eliminate them altogether once the dog's natural keenness to learn is aroused. If the dog is consistently rewarded in this manner you will never be quite sure whether he is responding because he has learned the command or whether he wants the tidbit. Some dogs may hurry through an exercise, giving a sloppy performance, just for the anticipated reward. This, of course, is unsatisfactory.

Once your dog begins to respond routinely to his commands, never allow him to respond sloppily. He must fully perform the requested behavior as he was taught. Bright dogs tend to test their masters now and then, just to see how much they can get away with. You will earn his respect by being firm and consistent with him. However, when correction is called for do not go too far and physically hurt or humiliate the dog. Such behavior is destructive not only to the learning process but also to the entire pet/owner relationship.

Another simple skill to teach the puppy is to follow you. This will not only bond the two of you as partners but will get him to really enjoy your company. Begin by following *him* wherever he goes, treating this as a game. As soon as he starts to move toward you, entice him into following you around the house. Frequently stop and start to keep things interesting. This simple skill will later aid in teaching the dog to walk easily on a leash and to heel at your side.

TRAINING TO LEAD

The leash is a fundamental tool in the training process. One of the first things you must do is let your dog become familiar with his collar and leash. Choose a collar that fits—not one he will grow into. Slip it over his neck and pet him reassuringly. When he has gotten used to it, tie a short piece of rope or cloth to the collar to let him feel the slight tug of an attachment to the collar. If this goes well, remove the rope or cloth and attach a lightweight leash. At first, let him drag it around. Carefully monitor him, though, so that he does not get caught on anything.

144

Once he is not bothered by the presence of the leash, pick it up and loosely hold it. Try your familiar follow-the-leader game and see if he is bothered by the leash's weight. Getting him to move around in this manner should keep him from fearing the use of the leash and prepare him for the next stages, where pressure is applied and the leash becomes a tool of restraint.

The next step is to tie him for a short period. Choose a spot with which he is familiar and comfortable. Make sure there are not items he can tangle with and choke himself on. Leave him alone for a short time, several times a day. At first he may whine and try to break away. If he gets unruly, calm him but do not release him. After several unsuccessful attempts at getting away, he will learn that the leash means he is no longer free to do as he pleases. At this point it becomes a training aid. Be sure to check the dog periodically, not only to verify his safety but to make sure he is not chewing on the leash. The leash is not a toy, it is a tool and a symbol of authority. If he should try to put the leash in his mouth, tell him "No" and mean it. If he persists, a slight upward tug will remove the leash from his mouth. You may want to consider using a light but sturdy metal leash until he no longer entertains the notion of chewing to rid himself of the leash.

The first few experiences at being tied should be kept very short, then very gradually increase the time he is tethered. Be sure to praise him for his good behavior each time you release him. You want him to adjust to this temporary constraint, not come to resent it.

Once he does not balk at your attaching the leash, you are ready to attempt a short walk on lead. Call him to your side, attach the leash to his collar, and move off. If he will not move, or if he pulls against the lead, continue to move and pull him along as best you can. Of course, do not allow him to hurt himself. If he lunges forward, straining the leash to get away, try to entice him back to your side or just hold him back as best you can. By continually applying pressure to his neck, he will have no choice but to learn that it is useless to struggle and that it is much more comfortable to walk than be pulled! Do not jerk him along, as this could injure his neck. When he gives up the struggle, reward him. Should he appear afraid, reassure him with praise and petting. Keep the first walks short and preferably in familiar terrain. Talk to him as you walk, in a low, friendly tone and pet him occasionally.

TRAINING TO SIT

This lesson should be taught indoors or in an area free from distractions (such as birds overhead, passing cars, children, etc.). The dog should be on lead and then he can be taught to sit in front of you or at your side. Place the leash in your right hand and hold it taut, with slight upward pressure. Give the command "Sit" and at the same time lean over with your left hand and press down on his rump until he is in the proper sitting position. Press steadily but not roughly. Once he is sitting, he may want to lie down or slide over on his side. Continue the upward pressure and straighten him up with your left hand. As soon as he is back in the proper position, praise him lavishly.

In the early lessons do not make him stay in the sit position for too long. Release the pressure from the leash and let him walk around a bit. After a minute or two, repeat the entire procedure. Use the same commands and actions, as this will help him understand what you are asking him to do. Be sure to reward him when he reaches the proper sit position, not when he breaks to get up. When he tries to break, tell him "No, Sit" and reposition him. Be clear, as he must learn to associate the reward with the sitting action.

Repeat the Sit lesson several times a day, but keep the initial lessons short and do not attempt more than five or six sits. As he progresses, exert less and less pressure on his rump each time. Eventually he will associate the command with the pressure, whether you actually apply it or not, and he will drop into the proper position at the sound of the command. Once this occurs, you can try to have him remain in the position for more than a few seconds, but not until he becomes distracted. When he stays for these short instances, praise him with "Good dog" and some petting. This is the first step in teaching him the Stay.

146

Ch. Lucene's Laura, C.D., bred and owned by Michelle Sudninski. Photo courtesy of Vivian Peters.

TRAINING TO STAY

Once your dog is responding perfectly to the Sit, place him in this position but retain a slight pressure from the lead on his neck. Gradually back away from him, only a foot or so at first; this time command him to "Stay." As you begin to move, simultaneously swing your hand forward toward his face, with the palm and fingers pointing down. Stop short of touching his nose. This hand signal should always be done at the instant you command him to stay and begin to move away from him.

Upon seeing you move, your dog will probably try to move toward you or to lie down. As soon as he breaks the position, return him to the Sit in the original location and repeat the entire Stay command. Be patient. While this lesson should be learned pretty easily, it is natural for the dog to be confused at first. Have the dog stay for a few seconds at first and increase the time gradually. At the end of each Stay, praise him profusely for a job well done.

It will take many repetitions for you to reliably expect your dog to stay for any length of time. Continue to drill him daily and you will eventually be able to have him remain still for up to thirty minutes, even with you out of sight.

TRAINING TO COME

Once your puppy knows his name, there should be little difficulty in getting him to come when called. As a puppy, he may be slow to respond, since a myriad of things may have his attention. The importance of this command is to teach the dog that he *must* respond when called, at once, regardless of where he is or what he is doing. The Come can be a life-saving command when used to extricate the dog from a dangerous situation.

You will need a large area for practicing this command and a light check cord of approximately twenty feet. Attach the cord to his collar and let him move about in the area. When you see that he is occupied with something, call him by name and command him to "Come." If he responds, praise him, and let him return to his romp. Repeat the command at various intervals. Most likely, he will tire of being interrupted and sooner or later will not respond. At this point, grasp the check cord, repeat the Come command, and give him a jerk. If he still does not respond properly, repeat the command and jerk several times. Generally, this should be enough to get your point across; but if all fails, repeat the command and reel him in. Reward him when he arrives. After one or two more successful commands, end the lesson and let him enjoy some freedom.

This command can be repeated several times a day, but do not overdo it. Three or four comes per lesson are plenty. If you push him too far he may not leave your side after being called, since he feels he is just going to be called back as soon as he leaves. This is disheartening to the dog. The object is to make him come when he is needed, not to make him behave like a robot.

Under no circumstances should you ever punish the dog when he comes to you. If you catch him in a punishable act, *go to him* and correct him. Do not call him to you and then lower the boom. This will make him wary of answering the Come.

As your dog progresses in his obedience training, he may become proficient at performing without the leash. You should never attempt off-leash work until you are certain that he can be trusted implicitly, and even then you should always begin this work in a confined area, such as a fenced yard. As previously mentioned, many dogs like to test their owners from time to time to see what they can get away with, and having him pull such a trick in an open area could be disastrous. With patience and a lot of work, you can eventually teach your dog to work off the leash and to respond to a whistle or hand signals—it all depends on how much time and effort you wish to put into the training process.

TRAINING TO DOWN

Like the Come, the Down can be a life-saving command if the dog gets himself into trouble. However, it is generally used when you just want to keep the dog in check.

After he has mastered the Sit, the Down should not be hard to teach. Place him in the sit position, and as you command him to "Down" use your right hand to pull his front feet out from under him and thereby cause him to slide down. Another method is to place the leash under your foot, making it taut. Press on his shoulders as you give the command. You want him to be on all fours, not spread out and relaxed; so, put him into the proper position if he should get too comfortable.

Ultimately you want to release him from the Down with an upward movement of the hand. At first you may call "Up" with a wave of the hand to startle him into movement. The Down, as well as the Sit, can be used with the Stay to keep the dog restrained for a length of time up to thirty minutes. Many owners and trainers feel that it is good discipline training if you practice a long Down Stay each day. This will be a valuable aid when you need a length of time where you know the dog is under constraint and not under foot.

TRAINING TO HEEL

Even if advanced obedience training is not one's goal, everyone wants his dog to walk nicely at his side when out for a stroll. This is known as the Heel. The dog should always be positioned to walk on your left side with his chest in line approximately with your knee. The reason for placing the dog on your left is because you thus maintain the most control, positioning

Two highly-trained dogs, a Rottweiler and an American Pit Bull Terrier, both in the "Down-stay" command.

yourself between the dog and any possible danger.

Hold the leash in your right hand at first and use the left hand to apply pressure on the leash and thereby control the dog's speed. Give the command "Heel" and walk at your regular pace. Try to keep him in line, applying a tug if he lags behind. Should he try to run ahead of you, first try a jerk of the leash to slow him down and return to the proper position. If this does not work and he continues to surge ahead, stop and place him in a Sit. Once he is patiently waiting, move out again, commanding him to "Heel" as he is released from the Sit. This stop-and-start process should get the point across to him very quickly that he is to move next to you, not out front or behind.

Keep the first lessons short, no more than ten or fifteen minutes. Any longer and he may grow tired or disinterested in going out for such excursions, especially if he is being placed in corrective sits.

150

TEACHING GOOD MANNERS

Aside from knowing the basic commands, your dog must be taught to control himself in all social situations. While no one wants a dog who acts like a shrinking violet or an overtrained robot, everyone wants a friendly companion who can be trusted to be on his good behavior, regardless of the situation and with little prodding from his owner.

Jumping Up. The overly exuberant dog greets all visitors or returning members of the household with a heartfelt welcome that includes his trying to jump into their arms. This practice should be discouraged when the tendency first begins to manifest itself, and there are several methods of correction.

The first method is to make the dog uncomfortable when he jumps up by holding on to his paws and making him remain with his two front legs in the air. Hold firmly but not so tightly as to cause the dog pain. You just want to frustrate him to the point where he can think of nothing else but getting his paws back on the ground. Speak to him, saying "No Jump" when you seize his paws. Repeat this procedure each time he jumps up and he will soon tire of the habit.

Another popular method is to raise your knee in response to his jumping, using it as a barrier that meets his chest and forces him back to the ground. While this is often successful, it can be harmful in that you can possibly injure the dog by applying too much force. Some dogs actually become more excited by the rejecting force of the knee and lunge forward even more vehemently in response. Used correctly, this method is a quick way to ward off the jumping dog by placing a barrier that puts him off balance and gets him quickly back on the ground. Always couple the knee-to-the-chest motion with a "No Jump" command.

If all else fails, try the water pistol method. Keep a loaded water pistol near the dog and squirt him in the face each time he jumps up on someone entering your home, telling him "No Jump." The dog finds this most displeasing and may quickly discard the jumping habit.

Rodsden's Majestic was Vivian Peters' first Rottweiler obtained as a pup from Rodsden's Rottweilers in 1968. She was shown and pointed but broke her leg and didn't move well after that. She was OFA-certified and had one litter of six pups, three of which later became champions. (Later she was infertile due to a uterine infection.) Fred McNabb of Golden West acquired her for security training along with two of her sons.

Barking. While you do not want to rid the dog of barking altogether—as this is often good security protection for the household—you do not want a dog that barks uncontrollably out of loneliness, boredom, or in response to common noises such as the doorbell or telephone. When such noises occur, allow the dog a bark or two and then reprimand him, saying "No Bark" and jerk him on his collar. Through constant repetition of this formal correction you should be able to break the dog of the habit. If not, more dramatic measures are called for.

Squirt the dog in the face with water from a water pistol each time he barks incessantly, saying "No Bark." You must be sure to act swiftly, as he must associate the onset of barking with water in the face. Keep a water pistol loaded and in a handy location.

152

Some dogs can be broken of the barking habit by scolding and placing the dog in isolation, such as a small room. Others will learn quickly if they are met with a large splash of water in the face. Some, however, require drastic action. If this is the case, an electric shock collar can be purchased to quickly break the habit, but this should be used only in extreme cases and for a very limited time by people who know what they're doing.

Always investigate the source of your dog's barking before you give him the command to stop barking. A dog's ears are very sensitive and he may be responding to a situation that you are not aware of. Barking should be discouraged only when the dog does it to excess or for no constructive purpose.

Chasing Cars. The habit of chasing cars is often fatal to dogs so prone, and it puts motorists in jeopardy as well, as they can lose control of their automobiles in attempting to deal with the dog. Chasing cars is a habit best broken by not allowing the dog to roam free, but some dogs even try to take off after the cars while on leash or chained in the yard.

If the dog attempts to chase a car while under restraint, react immediately to his attempts, sharply jerking him by the collar and saying "Stop" or "No!" You must then begin practice sessions to rid him of the habit. Walk him near the streets and await his lunges. Corrections must be very quick and very firm. You may want to set a trap for him by arranging with several friends to drive slowly past the dog. Should the dog attempt to go after the car, have the passenger-side occupant drop a bucket of water on his head. This should jolt him out of the desire to chase cars.

Pomac's Lexa P. Van Lare at fifteen months. Greg and Lori Benkiser, owners.

154

Chapter 9

Advanced Obedience Training and Competition

Just today, I saw a young fellow with a backpack place that pack on the sidewalk in front of a bookstore. He had with him a fine-looking Doberman Pinscher that was unusually large, especially for a Doberman, and he put the dog in a "Sit" guarding the backpack while he went into the bookstore to browse for fifteen minutes or so. Even though I have seen the same thing done many times with many different breeds, I was impressed, and you could tell that other people were too. For one thing, this was a very crowded area, as the bookstore was in a shopping center, and cars were whizzing all around. If the Doberman's training had not been certain, the dog would have been in danger, as just a few steps would have taken him into the path of a careening vehicle. Then, too, the owner had to have faith in the dog's stability of temperament, as some people walked nearby, although many others were giving him a wide berth. (No one made a move for the backpack, though!) It is impressive to be able to achieve something like that with one of the protection breeds. It's impressive with any breed; however, it might be a mistake with one of the smaller and less assertive breeds. If someone took a fancy to the backpack, they might just take it

155

and the dog too! I was almost certain that the Doberman guarding the backpack had been trained in an obedience class or had been trained by an owner who had learned how to train dogs in such a class.

Obedience trials, sanctioned by both the American Kennel Club and the United Kennel Club, are a form of competition for which the Rottweiler acquits himself admirably. If you are interested in entering your dog in this type of activity, you may be interested in knowing something about the history of the obedience movement.

Before dogs were bred for conformation and exhibited in shows, they were bred pretty much for function. As a matter of fact, the first conformation shows were started in Great Britain by gundog enthusiasts. They already had their retrievers, pointers, and flushing dogs, and they decided to have an additional competition for them: one based on appearance, with a written standard for each breed. Later, people with other dogs (that were not hunting dogs) wanted to show their charges as

Von Staten Rhapsody In Blue pictured at five months. By Am. and Vnz. Ch. Graudstark's Kona, C.D. ex Ch. Graudstark's Rhapsody. Owner: Virginia Koerber.

well. The sportsmen who had started the conformation shows were obliging, and they opened up a category under which these non-hunting dogs could be judged; that category was called "Nonsporting." In other words, there were the hunters' dogs, the "Sporting Group," and there was the "Nonsporting Group," which meant "all the rest!" Eventually, other classifications, or show groups, were added: a "Hound Group" (to encompass a different type of hunting dog), a "Terrier Group," a "Toy Group," a "Working Dog Group" (to which the Rottweiler is assigned), and a "Herding Group." These groupings have not been the most perfect solution, as some dogs have been placed in the wrong group because of misunderstandings, while others could fit in more than one group. But the system has satisfied most people and has not been set permanently in cement, as just recently the last group mentioned above has been formed. This Herding Group was originally part of the Working Group, but for a variety of reasons it was decided to give the herding dogs a classification of their own.

Since show dogs tended to be selectively bred to a standard of perfection, there was a tendency, sometimes, to breed exclusively for appearance. For that reason, one would often hear that show dogs were "all beauty but no brains!" In reaction to that, a performance competition was started in England and eventually found its way to the United States. These competitions were termed "obedience work," and the American Kennel Club cautiously issued permission to the Obedience Test Club of New York to stage two trials in 1934. The approved rules that were used for the trial were so satisfactory that only minor revisions were made until 1947 when some major changes were adopted.

The first trials had only an "Open class," but the next year a "Novice class" was added. At this writing, there are five classes in the trials, but there are only three divisions of work: the Novice, which leads to the Companion Dog degree; the Open, which leads to the Companion Dog Excellent appellation; and the Utility, by which a dog earns the Utility Dog degree. The Novice A and the Open A classes are for dogs of any breed and of either sex, and the entries must be handled by the dog's owner, not by a professional handler. In fact, a professional handler may not even handle his *own* dog in such a class. The Novice B and Open B classes are for dogs of any breed and of either sex, and they may be entered by any person, amateur or professional. You can compete with your dog in the Novice A or B until he has acquired the Companion Dog degree, when you must shift to the Open A or B classes, depending upon your dog's classification. After a dog has acquired the Companion Dog Excellent degree, you may choose between going on to the Utility classes, in which the amateurs and professionals compete on even terms, or you can continue to compete in Open B for as long as you wish. The same rule applies to Utility. Once a dog has been awarded that degree, he may compete indefinitely in both Utility and Open B.

In the Novice A and B classes, which lead to the Companion Dog degree, a dog must earn a total of at least 170 points in three trials (under three different judges) with at least six dogs competing in each of the three trials. It is not necessary that your dog win the trial, but he must score the 170 points in order to make progress toward the degree. Incidentally, the 170 points must be earned in the proper proportion; that is to say, at least half the value of *each* of the six exercises must be gained for a combined total of 170.

A description of the activities in each class may be of interest. In the Novice class, the first exercise is *heel on leash and figure eight,* which has an evaluation of 40 points. The handler may give the command "Heel!" and use the dog's name at the start of this and other exercises, but he may not give other commands or signals and must not operate with a tight leash. The judge's commands are: "Forward," "Halt," "Right turn," "Left turn," "About turn," "Slow," "Normal," and "Fast." At the conclusion of the first portion of the exercise, the judge says, "Exercise finished." Then the figure eight is executed with two stewards as the turning posts. The handler may praise or pet his dog and make ready for starting the new exercise.

The second exercise is the *stand for examination,* which carries

Four-month-old Angus vom Hochfeld, owned by Mike Howard, starts his show training. Photo courtesy of Vivian Peters.

a value of 30 points. The handler stands the dog for examination and moves in front of him to the end of the lead. The judge then goes over the dog, but not as carefully as in a breed (show) examination. He then orders the handler back to his dog, which he does by going around the dog and to its left side, and then commands, "Exercise finished." The dog must show no shyness, resentment, or movement during the stand for examination.

The third exercise is the off-leash work, referred to as *heel free*, except that there is no figure eight in this section in the Novice class. As in the heel on leash exercise, all movements are the same but without the leash to control the dog. The heel free is worth 40 points.

The *recall* is the fourth exercise, and it can provide 30 points. The handler sits the dog at a spot designated by the judge and moves as far away from the dog as the judge states, about 35 feet. On command the handler calls his dog in by calling "Come, Jack!" (or whatever the dog's name is). Alternatively, he may silently signal the dog, but he may *not* signal the dog *and* call him by name (or use any verbal command). The dog must respond promptly, sit directly in front of the handler, and, at the judge's command, swing around to heel position (seated).

The *long sit* is for one minute and the *long down* is for three minutes. During these last two exercises, the handlers are stationed across the ring from the dogs. (There may be several dogs in the ring for this event.) Steadiness in position counts here, and the dog may not shift until the judge says "Exercise finished." (In the case of the long down, the judge says "Down your dog," and then declares "Exercise finished.") The score for each of these exercises is 30 points, making the grand total in the Novice class 200 points for a perfect score.

TEST	MAXIMUM SCORE
1. Heel on Leash and Figure Eight	40 Points
2. Stand for Examination	30 Points
3. Heel Free	40 Points
4. Recall	30 Points
5. Long Sit	30 Points
6. Long Down	30 Points
MAXIMUM TOTAL SCORE	200 Points

In the Open class (including both A and B), *Heel free and figure eight* is the first exercise and 40 points can be earned. The calls of the judge are the same as in the Novice class heel on leash and figure eight, except the dog is off leash. Here, too, the handler may give only the one command at the start and may, at the command, "Exercise finished," praise and touch his dog.

Next is the *drop on recall* which is worth 30 points. The dog is set at one end of the ring and the handler sent to the other. The judge orders, "Call your dog," and signals the handler when to "drop" (to a down position) the oncoming dog by signal or voice command. Then the dog is called to a sit position before the handler. The judge orders, "Finish," and the dog is supposed to go smartly to the heel position (on command or signal of the owner), and the judge says "Exercise finished."

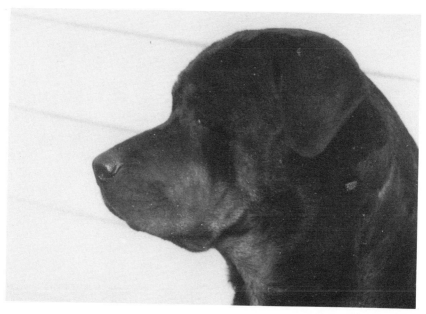

Nice head study of Ch. Inner Sanctums Oh Jezebel, C.D., pictured at fifteen months. By Am. and Can. Ch. Graudstark's Pegasus, C.D. ex Inner Sanctums Phoebe. Greg and Lori Bensiker, Van Lare Rottweilers, owners.

Now comes the *retrieve on flat*, and this requires the handler to throw a dumbbell at least twenty feet. (The dumbbells, hurdles, and all other apparatus for obedience trials are of a size that correspond to the size of the dog performing the exercise.) The dog must stay until asked by the judge to get (via an order to the handler) the dumbbell. The dog returns with the dumbbell and sits before the handler until the judge tells the handler, "Take it." The dog is then ordered to the heel position. This exercise can earn 20 points.

The *retrieve over high jump* exercise can earn 30 points. This requires the dog to stand steady as the handler throws the dumbbell over the high jump, which is set to one and one-half the height of the dog at the withers. Upon command of the judge, the dog is sent for the dumbbell. He must go over the jump, pick up the dumbbell, and return over the jump to the handler and sit before him. The judge will order, "Take it," and the handler takes the dumbbell and brings his dog to heel.

The *broad jump* comes next and is worth 20 points for a perfect performance. The hurdles are arranged in a series of four for larger breeds and reduced proportionately for the small ones. The spread of the boards is not to exceed six feet, and the average is not to be more than three times the height of the dog at the withers. The dog must remain sitting until he is directed to jump.

Thirty points can be earned in a perfect exercise of the *long sit*. This calls for a three-minute stay. The *long down* calls for a five-minute stay in the prone position for another 30 points. In both these exercises, at least six dogs must be in the class, and the dogs must sit or down without moving while the handlers are out of sight of the dogs.

TEST	MAXIMUM SCORE
1. Heel Free and Figure Eight	40 Points
2. Drop on Recall	30 Points
3. Retrieve on Flat	20 Points
4. Retrieve over High Jump	30 Points
5. Broad Jump	20 Points
6. Long Sit	30 Points
7. Long Down	30 Points
MAXIMUM TOTAL SCORE	200 Points

In the Utility class, there are six exercises for the 200 points that can be garnered by perfect execution.

In the *signal exercise*, the judge uses signals for directing the handler to signal his dog to drop, to sit, to come, and, finally, to finish. The entire routine is worth 40 points. Orders are the same as those described in the heel on leash and figure eight exercise (in the Novice class), with the dog off leash, of course; the commands "Stand your dog" and "Leave your dog" are, however, added to this exercise. The handler must not speak to his dog at any time while both are performing but must, instead, use hand signals.

In the next two Utility exercises, *scent discrimination (article no. 1)* and *scent discrimination (article no. 2)*, the dog must select, by scent alone, an article which has been handled by his handler and placed among other similar articles. The handler presents ten articles to the judge, one set of five identical objects not more than six inches in length made of rigid metal and the other set of five identical objects (again, not more than six inches in length) made of leather. The articles in each set are legibly numbered, each with a different number. The judge then designates one from each set and makes a written note of the numbers of the two articles he has selected. The handler holds the two articles, one at a time, and rubs the scent from his hands on them. The metal item is grouped with the others of its kind and each is placed on the ground randomly; the same is done with the leather item. The dog is required to retrieve the object that has his owner's scent on it; he then retrieves the other object in the same manner. Each scent discrimination exercise is worth 30 points, for a total of 60.

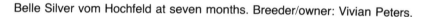

Belle Silver vom Hochfeld at seven months. Breeder/owner: Vivian Peters.

Von Staten Fantaisia, a three-and-one-half-month-old owned by Virginia Koerber.

In the *directed retrieve*, the handler provides the judge with three gloves. Each glove is then strategically placed on the ground at the opposite end of the ring and designated one, two, and three, reading from left to right. The judge gives the order "One," "Two," or "Three" and the handler gives his dog (by means of a single motion of the left hand) the direction to the designated glove, along with the command to retrieve. The dog is required to retrieve the glove and complete the exercise as in the retrieve on flat exercise (in the Open class). The maximum number of points that can be won in this directed retrieve exercise is 30.

164

In the *directed jumping* exercise, 40 points is the prize. A bar jump is placed on one side of the ring and a high jump on the other. The jumps are set at the required height for each dog, as described in the retrieve over high jump exercise in the Open class. The judge will designate which jump will be taken first, although both jumps must be taken to complete the exercise. The dog is set before the designated jump and commanded to stay as the handler takes a position to the side. The handler then commands "Over," and the dog is required to clear the hurdle and return, facing the handler. The judge will then say "Exercise finished" and begin the second part of the exercise with the question "Are you ready?"

The last Utility class exercise is the *group examination*. This is worth 30 points, and it is the one part of the class work in which all dogs of the class are in the ring together. The handlers leave their dogs on command from the judge, while he goes over all of them as though examining them for conformation show points. On completion, the judge calls the handlers back and declares the exercise finished.

TEST	MAXIMUM SCORE
1. Signal Exercise	40 Points
2. Scent Discrimination, Article No. 1	30 Points
3. Scent Discrimination, Article No. 2	30 Points
4. Directed Retrieve	30 Points
5. Directed Jumping	40 Points
6. Group Examination	30 Points
MAXIMUM TOTAL SCORE	200 Points

Tracking and Tracking Dog Excellent tests used to be part of the Utility Dog competition, but these are now separate competitions (or tests) of their own; however, once the degrees are earned, they are often affixed to the Utility Dog title. These, then, are the titles that can appear after the dog's name and what they mean:

C.D. (Companion Dog). This means that the dog has completed three tests in the Novice A or B classes, under at least three judges, and with at least six dogs in competition at each trial. In addition, a C.D. candidate must have made a score of 170 or better out of the possible 200 points. It also means that in each instance the dog has received at least fifty percent of the value of each individual exercise.

C.D.X. (Companion Dog Excellent). This attests to the fact that the dog, after first acquiring the C.D. degree, has completed three tests in the Open A or Open B classes, under at least three judges, and with at least six dogs in competition at each trial. He has made scores of 170 or better out of the possible 200 and in each case has received at least fifty percent of each individual exercise.

T.D. (Tracking Dog). This designation means that the dog, after acquiring at least the C.D. degree, has been rated "passed" by two judges officiating at the same time in an outdoor tracking test under rules set forth by the AKC.

U.D. (Utility Dog). This is the highest obedience degree. It signifies that the dog, having acquired the C.D. and C.D.X. degrees, has completed three tests in the Utility Class, under three different judges, and with three or more dogs in competition has made scores of 170 or better of the possible 200 and has received each time at least half of the valuations allowed in each individual exercise.

U.D.T. (Utility Dog Tracker). This simply means that a dog has all the obedience degrees and has passed the tracking test too, according to the rules of the AKC.

As you may have noticed, I have spent a considerable amount of relative space on the obedience competitions. If the reader were to guess that I consider these activities especially important for the Rottweiler, the reader would be absolutely correct. For the Rott is a large and powerful animal, one of the most powerful of dogs, and fearless by nature. It has not happened yet, at this writing, but let's hope that our Rottweiler doesn't come under attack in the same way the Bull Terrier breeds have, with many cities passing ordinances that prohibit them or severely restrict them. The best antidote for this scenario—and the best prevention—is to have a large number of Rottweiler owners interested in obedience. People will be less likely to give way to hysteria if these fearsome-looking beasts are flawless in deportment.

SCHUTZHUND TRIALS

For those who are unfamiliar with it, Schutzhund training involves three facets: tracking, obedience (including retrieving), and protection. It takes an exceptional dog to achieve a Schutzhund title and many hundreds of hours of work by a dedicated handler. Schutzhund originated in Germany over 75 years ago and was also the technique used to train war dogs. Now it is a sport, with control of the dog and temperament being very important. Schutzhund titles are confirmed by the United Schutzhund Clubs of America, and this organization works under the auspices or guidance of the original Schutzhund Club in Germany.

For people who are interested in training their own dogs in protection work on a competitive basis, the various Schutzhund clubs offer a wonderful opportunity to accomplish this. Again, you can find out about local Schutzhund clubs and competitions from other dog people in your area or from that old standby, your local professional boarding kennel. We will talk more about training your own dog for protection work in the next chapter.

WEIGHT COMPETITIONS

If your dog is not a good show specimen or if you, yourself, are not inclined toward that type of competition, you may want to try him in weight-pulling competitions. This is something that has only recently become popular, but the Rottweiler should be especially suitable for such events, given his past history as a cart-pulling dog. There are two organizations that are currently sanctioning such competitions. One is the International Sled Dog Racing Association (ISDRA), and the other is the American Dog Breeder's Association. The two organizations have a different set of rules for weight-pulling contests; however, the primary difference is that the ISDRA utilizes sleds for the weight that the dog pulls, while the American Dog Breeder's

A 1971 photo of Ch. Kleinste Bettina of Fair Lane, C.D. pictured at one-and-one-half years. Breeder: Vivian Peters. Owners: Gordon and Dirkje Watt.

Association utilizes carts, sometimes on rails.

People who don't know any better think of weight competitions as being cruel, but the dogs that do well in them seem to enjoy the sport; in fact, I've never seen a dog entered that didn't seem to enjoy himself—even if he was eliminated early. The handlers of the dogs don't like them to have a feeling of having failed, so when they see that a particular dog is not going to be able to pull the weight within the specified time limit, they get in back of the load and "help" the dog. (The handler, thus, fouls out, but the dog thinks that he has made the pull.) All the dogs seem to enjoy this competition, and the ones that do well *really* enjoy it. The dogs at least are getting attention and an outing (in addition to the fact that they had to have regular conditioning to be a serious contender at a weight pull). The more time you spend with your dog doing something you both enjoy, the closer will be your relationship and the happier you'll both be.

If you decide to become involved in this type of competition, you'll need to check with dog people or boarding kennels to find

168

out if there are some type of weight-pull competitions being held in your area. You'll need to find out if your dog has the desire and aptitude for pulling. It will be necessary to get him used to the harness. (Once you've made contact with weight-pull organizations, you can determine where to get proper harnesses.) After your Rottweiler is used to the harness, have him pull some very light loads at first. Gradually build up to heavier loads. A good procedure would be to start out with a small cart or a child's wagon (empty) and let him have several days of just pulling that and getting used to the wagon and the idea of pulling. You may wish to have pulling sessions daily, but three times a week is sufficient. Build him up to the weights very slowly. Once you get him up to fairly high weights, you may wish to have a practice contest occasionally. Have him make several pulls, utilizing relatively light weights at first, just as you would in a real contest. Then gradually increase the weights, and praise him highly when he pulls the weight past the marker. Regardless of how light the weight is, make him feel that he has really accomplished something each time he does it. Be sure to have a friend ready to "help" the dog in case he falters. Remember, easy does it. You don't want to progress too swiftly, as "burnout" is always a problem with physical competitions with dogs (or humans!)

Some trainers believe that the Rottweiler is one of the few breeds in which a female pup is likely to be a good protection dog prospect. This loyal fifteen-month-old bitch, Ch. Inner Sanctums Oh Jezebel, C.D. owned by Greg and Lori Benkiser, has already shown her prowess in obedience.

Chapter 10

Perfecting the Protector

While I said that we would talk about training your own dog for protection, I would be remiss if I did not warn that probably ninety percent of such efforts are unsuccessful. While dog training is based on scientific principles, it remains basically an art. The really good trainer knows, seemingly from intuition, but in actuality probably from long experience with dogs and an aptitude for working with them, exactly what course of action to take *with a particular dog* and *in a particular set of circumstances.* Even if you think you know dogs, you may find yourself perplexed or hard pressed to solve a particular problem. Even worse, you may make a horrendous error that ruins the dog for protection work. Now a large number of Rottweiler experts feel that the breed is a natural protection dog and needs no training. In fact, some of them are dead set against protection training for a Rott. They feel that the balance between appropriate aggression and indiscriminate attacks is just right in the breed. They feel, perhaps, that he is far too formidable a beast to be stoking the fires of his aggression. All these people have a point; however, every breed, including the Rottweiler, has a variation in temperament. For that reason, you can't be certain that your own personal dog will be a natural protector. To be safe, it is best to have him trained. And, if the dog has the training and doesn't work out as a protection dog, at least you've found that fact out before it is too late (i.e., when a burglar enters the house and the dog does nothing!).

If you decide you want a protection-trained dog, you might consider once again the idea of getting a grown, trained dog. Remember, the advantages are that you know you have a bona fide protection dog. In addition, there is no time-loss factor; the dog is able to go to work almost immediately. With a puppy, all the time he is growing up, you are without protection; and then, if he doesn't turn out to be a protection dog, you're "stuck" with a dog to whom you most likely have become quite attached. Then, if you decide to get a professionally-trained adult dog, you most likely will have to get rid of the dog you already have (if both dogs are males), as two strange male dogs are not likely to get along together in the same house. There are a few disadvantages in buying a trained dog, however. First, there is the high cost, already mentioned earlier. Then there is a break-in period. Even though a dog has been trained to commands, there still is the possibility of problems. For example, you suddenly have to retrain your best friends not to just walk nonchalantly into your house! You see, if you want your dog to prevent undesirable people from entering your home, either when you're there or away, then you're going to have to teach your neighbors and friends to ring the doorbell and wait until you actually go to the door to let them in. Otherwise the dog may become confused and decide he isn't there for protection work after all.

In any case, unless the trained dog is exceptionally aggressive, he probably won't start working for you for about two weeks, or possibly longer. He has to learn that your home is his home, and he has to let his confidence build up in new surroundings and new people. Before he becomes bonded to you and members of your family, he may feel no urge to protect you or your property. No reputable trainer, however, will send you away with a trained protection dog without having spent a good deal of time working with you and your dog.

Titan, in training to become a police dog, guards a "prisoner."

Now seems like a good time to sort out some of the terms we have been using here and to see just what is meant by protection dog. While I use the term "guard dog" in the way it was used in my youth, its connotation today is more along the line of a "junkyard dog," just a mean, ill-tempered dog that is a menace to anyone other than his owner. Then there are "attack dogs." These are police dogs that are trained to work with a handler. Left to their own devices, these dogs respond to all threats equally, and for that reason, these are not dogs for families to own. A dog that is selected and trained for "protection" work is different. He is trained to respond to provocational threats by attack, if necessary. If you, or members of your family, are being threatened, or the house is being invaded, the protection dog will go into action as an independent, defensive weapon.

Anyway, for now, let us assume that you've decided to take your chances with a pup, gambling that he will turn out to be exactly what you want in the way of a guard—oops, I mean protection—dog. We've already talked about selecting a pup by studying pedigrees and by studying the litter itself and picking out a

173

self-assured pup. As a reminder, the Rottweiler is one of few breeds—some trainers list only two—in which a female pup is likely to be a good protection prospect, so your own personal preference can guide you there. I would suggest that if you don't have your pup professionally trained, you, yourself, should at least get into a class (much like an obedience class) for owners to learn to train their dogs. Unlike obedience classes, these are not always free, unless they are sponsored by some group, such as your local Schutzhund club or perhaps even a breed club. Knowing what I do about the training involved in the development of protection dogs, I am not inclined to have you attempt it yourself—even if you have an entire book on the subject. Still, even if you are going to do the training on your own, under guidance and supervision, you might be interested in the general approach to the training.

TRAINING METHODS

Basically, there are two schools of thought on the training of a protection dog. One is the "prey" method. In this method a lure is used (from puppyhood) to entice the dog to attack. Lots of tug-of-war play is involved in this method, and it eventually leads to the dog's attacking the "sleeve" (a piece of padded equipment) of an agitator. At first, the agitator will give only passive resistance to the dog tugging on the sleeve, mainly showing submission to give the dog confidence. One problem with this method that many trainers point out is that dogs thus trained often become "sleeve happy." That is to say, they direct their attack at the padded sleeve of the agitator to the extent that the agitator can throw down the sleeve and the dog will attack that, completely ignoring the man.

We will concentrate on the other method, sometimes called the "socialization" method. A pup is taken home at eight weeks of age and exposed to all of the elements of socialization that we talked about earlier. However, when he reaches the age of six months, we begin to discourage people who are not members of the immediate family from petting him or playing with him. This is an attempt to develop a neutral attitude toward

This dog has been given the command "Out," which means he is to discontinue the attack. At this stage of his training, he is slow to respond to the command.

The dog is under no command here, but he is attentive to any "suspicious" behavior by the agitator.

strangers. He will tolerate being petted but will not seek their attention. When the dog gives a warning bark at a strange noise or someone at the door, he is rewarded by lavish praise. It is a good idea to establish the rule that no one comes into your home with an automatic welcome unless you go to the door and let the person in. That is the signal to the dog that the person is a welcome visitor and is not to be given any further attention.

WORKING WITH AN AGITATOR

Many trainers believe it is good to let the pup watch other dogs working with an agitator. It was once believed that dogs could not learn from example; however, this belief has been modified to a degree. When the dog is a year old, some light agitation can be introduced; in fact, even prior to this time, some very light agitation can be utilized. This would consist of having a friend sneak around the property at a considerable distance from the house. When the pup barks or advances a wee bit, the "agitator" scurries away. Agitation training consists of having a stranger intrude on a dog's property, the yard, or the owner's car. The intrusion has to be very light at first, always making sure that the young dog is never intimidated; in fact, the opposite is desired: we are trying to build up confidence in the dog. An important indicator is the tail. A tail that is upright, and preferably wagging, is a good sign. Some people might be surprised by the statement, as most of us think of a dog with a wagging tail as being in a greeting mood. While it's true that a wagging tail is like a person's smile and is, thus, usually a friendly gesture, it can also be an indicator of excitement or pleasure. When the dog's confidence is sufficiently built up, the agitator can approach more closely and make mildly threatening moves. For example, he may strike at you or in the direction of the dog. Keep your dog on a leash, in this case, to keep the agitator from being bitten. Of course, there are complete protection outfits which the agitator can wear, but these have two drawbacks. One is that they are quite expensive, and the other is that a dog may only respond to an agitator in such garb if that is the only way he has been trained. It is best to have people the dog doesn't know

176

work as the agitators, and it would be very desirable to have more than one agitator. Never be the one to agitate your own dog. This should be self-evident to a dog person, but a surprising number of people have done this. Such an action thoroughly confuses the dog and quite possibly makes a complete game out of the entire training . . . and this is a real effort in futility!

After many weeks of light agitation, that is gradually built up to heavy agitation (whereby the agitator strikes out at the dog with a light stick and is then chased off by the leashed dog), some off-leash work may be introduced. In this case a muzzle must be used, and the dog should be accustomed to it under pleasant conditions, long before this exercise. When the dog is released upon the agitator (a good way to do this is to simply proceed as before, but let the leash drop at the height of the dog's excitement), the agitator will run away. When the dog hits him, no matter how lightly, he will fall down, hold his hands and arms away and act as if he is really being mauled. In the course of the training, the dog should have been taught to "out" or "drop" or whatever command you're going to use to get the dog to abort the attack. You utilize the command now and let the agitator skulk off. This procedure is continued for some time, with the agitator giving more and more resistance each time, as he sees that the dog can take it. Rottweilers can become so adept at working with a muzzle that they can subdue a strong man just with their wrestling ability. (That is one reason for teaching the out command first!)

Eventually, some sleeve work is necessary, as it teaches the dog to take hold and to work his hold. To keep the dog from becoming "sleeve happy," it is necessary to have an experienced agitator, and, as a matter of fact, a knowledgeable agitator is an important prerequisite in all the training. Since a Rottweiler is such a powerful animal, the agitator must be prepared for a charge that is similar to that of a freight train. The agitator must not take the charge to the sleeve full on. One way for him to avoid full force of the attack is to keep the sleeve hidden until the last moment; then, as he takes the blow, he lets the impetus of the charge pass off to the side. The agitator still will be taken to

Bethel Farm's Devil-May-Care, also known as "Bear," owned by Kevin and Diane Hartle.

the ground, but at least he won't feel as though he's just been hit by a pile driver!

Since we have emphasized the avoidance of a sleeve happy dog, it would be prudent to have the agitator in full protection dress in case the Rott doesn't take the sleeve. You can see that there is a delicate balance to be found between giving a dog a thorough work-out on the sleeve and having him become sleeve happy. There is also a balance to achieve between working the dog on a fully-protected agitator and having him lose interest in non-costumed (unprotected) people. And finally, there is a balance between a dog that is appropriately protective and one that is aggressive toward or unduly suspicious of *all* people. The point is to have a dog who is safe with anyone that does not constitute a danger to us.

It is my hope that all of the foregoing pointers will nudge you in the direction of utilizing the services of a professional trainer or a club with good, competent people as advisors. As you can see, training a protection dog is no simple matter. It is not difficult to have a dog that is aggressive to all people, but that can be tragic. Such a dog is only useful as a "junkyard dog" as we mentioned previously. It is also quite easy to have a dog that will never attack anyone; but, of course, he will not make a good protection dog. To produce the exact balance that we need in a protection dog is both an art and a science.

It may be that you will decide to take your chances and rely on the natural protective instincts of the Rottweiler breed. That is not the worst decision in the world, for the Rottweiler certainly does have this innate ability and many a Rottweiler devotee will insist that a Rott does not need protection training; in fact, some will be adamant that he should not have it at all. Well, maybe. But if you do go the route of relying on the breed's natural protection, I hope you will at least take him through a novice obedience class. That is good for the breed, it is good for you, and good for your dog. What's more, you'll find that you and your dog have become even closer friends.

Rodsden's Majestic at one year with her handler Dave Schneider in 1969. Owner: Vivian Peters. This lovely bitch is true proof that a well-bred Rottweiler can be all things—family friend, show dog, and working dog. Photo by Henry C. Schley.

Chapter 11

Showing Your Rottweiler

As the owner of a purebred dog, you can be proud of your breed's heritage and breed qualities. But owning a purebred is no guarantee that he is a top-quality specimen as compared to the breed's standard of perfection. The dogs that win Best In Show honors are very rare indeed and are often the products of years of breeding efforts by knowledgeable breeders. Show-quality specimens are generally hard to find and will usually carry a hefty price tag if purchased from a breeder, although a few "Cinderella" champions can be found now and then from novice breeders. If you are looking for a potential show dog, familiarize yourself with the requirements of the breed standard and scrutinize as many litters as possible before selecting your dog.

While the dream of seeing one's perfectly groomed dog gait proudly around the show ring on his way to being named Best In Show at a major competition is attainable only by a select few pedigreed dog owners, participation in some aspect of the show game can be available to many owners.

181

At the age of ten months, Ch. Bonnie of Fair Lane is shown taking a "major" from the Open Class, handled by Dave Schneider. Breeder/owner: Vivian Peters. Photo by Henry C. Schley.

Winning a five-point "major" owner/handled at fourteen months is Ch. Inner Sanctums Oh Jezebel, C.D. By Am. and Can. Ch. Graudstark's Pegasus, C.D. ex Inner Sanctums Phoebe. Owners: Greg and Lori Benkiser.

Ch. Hallmark's "The Sting" repeating her Best of Opposite Sex win of 1981 in 1982 at Westminster. She went on to become a No. 1 Top Producer for 1983. Owners: Patrick and Olga McDonald. Sired by Ch. Starkrest's Polo-R out of Ch. Radio Ranch's Echo v. Tanrich.

TYPES OF DOG SHOWS

There are several types of dog shows that offer various levels of competition for purebred dogs. Fun matches are often sponsored by local dog clubs and fanciers to offer interested owners a chance to try their hand at showing their dogs. These are often small shows with very modest entry fees that are collected at the door. The entered dogs may be judged in groups comprised of various breeds and both sexes. While various prizes and ribbons may be awarded, the real focus of this match show is to provide a fun time for all. Match shows give inexperienced handlers and their dogs a chance to gain ring poise and experience.

Sanctioned match shows are slightly more formal than fun matches, as they are run in accordance with the American Kennel Club guidelines. Your dog's success at a sanctioned match may be a good indicator of whether your dog may have a future in the show game. Although these matches offer no championship points, if your dog does well and places ahead of other entries of the same breed you might begin to seriously consider whether you want to take the next step up the show ladder—entering the championship shows.

Make the most of these match show experiences. As they are learning experiences, ask the judges for their opinion of your dog's chances and for an evaluation of your handling technique. Talk to the more experienced exhibitors for any tips or advice they may be able to give you. Not only beginners participate in match shows, as established kennels often enter their young dogs to acquaint the dogs with the show process. Match shows have much to offer aspiring competitors.

There are two types of shows where your dog can win points toward his championship title: all-breed shows and specialty shows. Specialty shows are limited to entries of one breed only, while all-breed shows are open to all AKC recognized breeds. An all-breed conformation show may be designated *benched* or *unbenched*. A benched show requires the dog to stay at his appointed bench area during the advertised hours of the show, although he may be removed to be taken to the exercise pen, to the grooming area (no more than one hour before his showing

Unable to attend Westminster in 1983, previous two-time Best of Opposite Sex winner Ch. Hallmark's "The Sting" was represented by her two sons, littermates Ch. Pomac's Yoda of Dagobah and Ch. Pomac's Graf Tanzer, who took Winners Dog and Reserve Winners Dog that year at the tender age of fifteen-and-a-half months. Yoda is owned by Patrick and Olga McDonald, Pomac's Rottweilers, and "Tan" is owned by Greg and Lori Benkiser of Van Lare Rottweilers.

time), or to the appropriate judging area. The famous Westminster Kennel Club show is an example of a benched show. At an unbenched show the dog is only required to be present at the time of his judging. At such shows the dog can be kept in the owner's crate or car or any appropriate location, and he may leave as soon as his judging is completed.

Junior Showmanship is another aspect of the show game that is open to young handlers only. In this competition children between the ages of ten and seventeen handle dogs owned by their immediate families. Junior Showmanship provides children with the opportunity to experience the feel of the show ring and to train themselves for actual breed competition. In this activity the handling skills of the Junior Showmanship competitors are judged, not the conformation quality of the dog (although he must be a purebred). The children are separated by age and

This magnificent male, Ch. Pomac's Yoda of Dagobah, truly exemplifies the beauty of the Rottweiler breed. He is shown here winning a five-point "major." Proudly owned by Patrick and Olga McDonald.

Ch. Der Catlin's H H Dieter, C.D., handled by Terry Gaskins. Breeder: Susan Catlin. Owner: Vivian Peters.

number of previous Junior Showmanship wins. The competitors are placed in divisions: Novice A for ten-to-twelve-year-olds who have not won three firsts in this class, Novice B for thirteen-to-sixteen-year-olds who have not won three firsts in this class, Open A for ten-to-twelve-year-olds who have won three firsts in Novice, and Open B for thirteen-to-sixteen-year-olds who, again, have won three Novice firsts.

Obedience trial competition is a very different type of show competition. As an obedience competitor, the dog is not judged on his appearance and conformation to the breed standard of perfection (although he must be purebred and registered with the AKC). Rather, he is judged on his ability to perform required activities and obey the commands of his handler. Obedience trials are often held in conjunction with all-breed or specialty shows or they can be held separately. Since obedience competition differs markedly from the conformation competitions, it has been discussed in detail in a separate chapter.

Pomac's Lexa P. Van Lare by Ch. Radio Ranch's Axel v. Notara ex Ch. Hallmark's "The Sting" pictured taking Reserve Winners Bitch at fifteen months of age. Owners: Greg and Lori Benkiser.

ATTAINING A CHAMPIONSHIP TITLE

While very few dogs ever attain Best In Show honors, the primary goal of most exhibitors is to have their dog reach his championship. This is generally regarded as the standard of conformation excellence. A championship title can be attained only by participation in sanctioned "point" shows—shows that award an appropriate number of championship points for placing first in the classes. The scale of points is determined by the number of dogs entered in the classes as compared to the minimum numbers of entries required by breed regulations for various point level wins. A win of three points is called a "major." To attain a championship title, a dog must accumulate at least fifteen points under at least three judges, and there must be two major wins from different judges included in the fifteen points. It is possible to receive fifteen or more points and not qualify for championship, as the major wins are lacking. A major win generally requires the dog to be of superior quality and to defeat a large number of entries at a large show.

During the judging each dog will be judged against his breed standard of perfection. This is a set of very exacting guidelines that has been drawn up by the national breed club and approved by the American Kennel Club. It defines point by point what a perfect specimen of the breed would look, move, and act like, including such details as the desired set of the teeth, texture of the coat, shape of the head, etc. Besides pointing out the ideal, the standard also defines which characteristics are considered to be faults or disqualifications.

THE CLASSES

If your purebred is registered with the American Kennel Club, he is eligible to compete in point shows as long as he is not altered (neutered) or somehow disqualified by breed rules. Depending on his age, sex, and number of previous show wins, there are various classes in which he can be entered: Puppy, Novice, Bred-by-Exhibitor, American-bred, and Open. These five classes are defined as follows:

PUPPY CLASS: Open to dogs at least six months of age but not more than twelve months of age.

NOVICE CLASS: Open to dogs six months of age or older that havenot won a first prize in any class other than Puppy Class and that have less than three first prizes in the Novice Class itself and no championship points. The class is limited to dogs whelped in the United States and Canada.

BRED-BY-EXHIBITOR CLASS: Open to all dogs, except champions, six months of age and over that are owned wholly or in part by the person or by the spouse of the person who was breeder or one of the breeders of record. The class is limited to dogs whelped in the United States or, if individually registered in The American Kennel Club Stud Book, for dogs whelped in Canada. Dogs entered in the Bred-by-Exhibitor Class must be handled by the breeder or one of the breeders of record or by a member of the immediate family of the breeder or one of the breeders of record. Members of an immediate family include husband, wife, father, mother, son, daughter, brother, or sister.

AMERICAN-BRED CLASS: Open to all dogs, except champions, six months of age or older that were whelped in the United States by reason of a mating that took place in the United States.

OPEN CLASS: Open to all dogs six months of age or older except in a member specialty club show held only for American-bred dogs, in which case the Open Class shall be only for American-bred dogs.

PREPARING FOR SHOW COMPETITION

Once you have located your show dog, or if you are lucky enough to own a puppy that is blossoming into a beautiful specimen and have received encouragement from judges at puppy matches about your dog's chances in championship competition, you must begin training yourself and your dog for the skills of the show ring. The best initial preparation is to visit a few

Ch. Der Catlin's H H Dieter, C.D., handled by Terry Gaskins, moves around the ring. Breeder: Susan Catlin. Owner: Vivian Peters.

Ch. Pomac's Graf Tanzer winning a Group Fourth his first time out over twenty-eight group entries. Owners: Greg and Lori Benkiser. Handled by Lori Benkiser.

shows and watch the goings on. Talk to the experienced exhibitors, as they are generally more than happy to extol the virtues of their breed and their particular dogs. If you plan on showing your dog yourself, study the movements of the professional handlers and their technique for controlling their dogs. Watch the judges to see what they require of the dogs and the handlers. Spending a few days mingling with the more experienced exhibitors may prove very helpful in acquiring a "feel" for the show ring.

During an actual judging, your dog will be required to gait around the show ring and be physically inspected by the judge. Before you enter any competition, train your dog to gait at a trot by your side. Teach him to hold his head high and move in a straight line. He must master this and perform it willingly to accentuate the beauty and grace of his movement, as this will be under the watchful eye of the judge.

The judge will want to closely examine the dog's physical structure. To do this, the dog will need to calmly stand for examination and allow the judge to run his hands over the dog's body. The judge will carefully feel the body contours and examine the teeth. Teach the dog to stand squarely with his head erect and the hind legs positioned slightly back. It is easiest to familiarize the dog to this position if you routinely "stack" or set him in this manner every time you groom him. He should learn to stay in this stacked position for at least two minutes.

Practice gaiting and stacking the dog as if you were in competition and the dog will quickly become accustomed to the procedure. If possible, have another person simulate the role of the judge by running his hands over the dog's body during your practice sessions. This will acquaint him with the feel of a stranger's touch. It is essential that the dog learn to be at ease during such examinations, as exhibiting any signs of aggression or biting during the judging will spoil any chance of show ring success.

Handling classes can be an aid for both handler and dog. Local dog clubs usually sponsor a series of classes run by a professional handler or a very experienced exhibitor to help novice exhibitors

Judging the Working Group at a conformation show. Photo courtesy of Vivian Peters.

correct any faults they may have in their showing technique. For a modest fee you can be critiqued on your strengths and weaknesses and instructed on how to highlight your dog's best features through good presentation. Handling instruction should not be confused with obedience instruction, as your dog should have mastered the basic obedience commands prior to his beginning any ring work. Instruction in handling is intended to help dog and owner become an efficiently working team—working *with,* not against each other.

ENTERING A DOG SHOW

When—and only when—you feel confident that both you and your dog have mastered the basic requirements for the ring, it is time to enter a point show. By reading the local dog club bulletins or the national dog publications you can find the location and dates of shows in your area. Write to the show superintendent or secretary listed with the show information

192

and he or she will supply you with the official entry form and all necessary applications. A listing of the American Kennel Club sanctioned point shows can routinely be found in such magazines as *Pure-bred Dogs/American Kennel Gazette, Dog World,* and *Dog Fancy.* Similarly, details which pertain to Canadian Kennel Club shows can be found regularly in the magazine *Dogs in Canada.*

Be sure to fill in the entry form accurately, as any mistake on official information may nullify the application. Decide which class your dog is to compete in. Novices with young dogs should begin in the Puppy Class and gradually move up the class ladder to the Open Class as handler and dog gain ring experience. Entries are generally limited to a certain number of dogs and usually close three weeks before the date of the show, so do not wait until the last moment to send in the application.

THE DAY OF THE SHOW

Before leaving for the show, be sure to pack all items you will need that day: a dog crate, water and food dishes, bottled water (to avoid a possible adverse reaction to different drinking water), food, a show lead, a chain or leash to tie him to his crate or bench area, and grooming tools. Check to see that you have in your possession the identification ticket sent to you by the show superintendent verifying your entry and stating your dog's judging time at the show. Review this information and plan your travel and arrival time accordingly.

As the trip in the car will be exciting for the dog, do not feed him the morning of the show. You may give him a dry dog biscuit or two or a very light meal if he appears hungry. Plan on giving him his main meal of the day after his judging, as a sated dog will not show as eagerly and enthusiastically as a slightly hungry one.

Upon arrival at the show, give the dog a drink of water and follow this with a trip to the exercise pen so that he can relieve himself. It is important the dog relieve himself before he is exposed to the excitement of the judging ring to avoid a possibly embarrassing ring experience.

Ch. Pomac's Graf Tanzer, shown by owner/handler Lori Benkiser to a Group Third. Owners: Greg and Lori Benkiser.

CLOTHING

It is important to dress the part of a dog show competitor. The emphasis should be on presenting a neat appearance while wearing clothes that are comfortable and allow you ease of movement. Shoes are especially important. Select a pair with rubber, nonslip soles and be sure they are comfortable enough to spend an active afternoon in.

Clothing should be appropriate for the occasion—neither too formal nor too informal. You should be able to gait with your dog around the ring without restriction from tight clothes. If possible, wear an outfit with a small pocket to hold small supplies or bait. Avoid clothing that is too loose and do not wear dangling jewelry, as these can be distracting to the dog while you both are in motion around the ring.

Color is also important, as you want to wear clothing that is not so dark that it easily displays hairs or dusty paw prints. Your clothing should blend, not distract, from the coloring of your

Ch. Scirocco's Secretariat standing proudly as the son of the top-winning Rottweiler in the United States for 1976, 1977, and 1978, Ch. Centurion's Che Von Der Barr. Patrick and Olga McDonald of Pomac Rottweilers, owners.

dog. You do not want to appear so similar in color that you merge together with your dog. As a rule, if you own a dark-colored dog you should wear clothing that is slightly lighter than his coat. This will set a pleasing contrast between owner and dog.

One last point to remember: be prepared for all types of weather, especially if you are attending an outdoor show. Always carry rain gear. Have a sweater or light jacket handy to add or take off as the conditions change.

IN THE RING

Once you have checked in with the steward and your class is called, take your place with the other competitors. Be sure that you have placed your arm band on your left arm, at the top so it can be easily seen by the judge and the steward.

Get in line and position yourself accordingly—not too close or too far from the other entries. Listen to the instructions of the judge and proceed as he or she requests. Both handler and dog are expected to conduct themselves in a "gentlemanly" fashion in the ring, showing courtesy not only to the judge but to the other competitors as well.

GAITING

One of the key aspects in the judging process is to review the dog's gait. The judge will ask the handler to move the dog around the ring to assess the dog's grace and ease of movement. The dog should always be placed on your left side, and you retain control by holding the leash in your left hand. It is imperative that you practice this action until you are sure the dog will remain under control during the actual judging process. This is an important maneuver, as it often imparts the first impression of your dog in the judge's mind.

There are several common patterns that the judges use to evaluate a dog's gait. The most common is to move the entire class of dogs under evaluation around the ring in a circular pattern, usually reversing the pattern after a revolution or two around the ring. The dog should be gaiting freely, on as loose a lead as possible.

During the individual examination of your dog the judge may ask you to gait the dog "out and back," in a "triangle," in the "circular" pattern, or in a pattern of his choice that he feels will give him the best view of those aspects of the gait that he cares to evaluate.

When moving the dog for the judge, the point to keep in mind always is to present the dog at his best. The dog should always be kept between you and the judge so that you do not obscure the judge's view. Control is of the utmost importance because it shows the judge that you and the dog are confident and well prepared for the show ring.

JUDGING PROCEDURE

The classes for the male dogs will be called first, in this order: Puppy, Novice, Bred-by-Exhibitor, American-bred, and Open. The winner in each class is selected and then competes for the Winners Dog title. Only the Winners Dog is awarded points toward his championship title, the number of points being decided by the number of dogs participating in the breed competition. The procedure is then repeated for the female entries. This time, the class winners compete for the title of Winners

Bitch. Reserve Winners Dog and Reserve Winners Bitch are also named at this point, but they do not receive any championship points.

Winners Dog and Winners Bitch then move on to compete against each other for Best of Winners. They are then placed against the Specials (champions) for the Best of Breed and Best of Opposite Sex to the Best of Breed titles. Best of Breed is the top breed award, and this winner goes on to represent the breed in the Group competition. At this level all Best of Breed winners from the specific groups are judged against their own breed standards and first, second, third, and fourth place winners are selected. These dogs are chosen by the judge as the best breed representatives and the first place winner moves on to represent his group in the Best In Show competition. From these Group winners (the Groups are Sporting breeds, Hound breeds, Working breeds, Terrier breeds, Toy breeds, Non-sporting breeds and Herding breeds) the judge selects one dog as the best specimen of the day—the Best in Show.

Handlers ready their dogs for the judge at an outdoor show. Photo courtesy of Vivian Peters.

ROTTWEILER STANDARDS

Show points are based on a breed standard. A breed standard gives a verbal picture of what the perfect specimen should look like. One of the problems of a standard is that no matter how well written it may be, it will still be subject to interpretation. That means that new generations of breeders can gradually change the appearance of the breed by interpreting the standard differently. For example, some of the old-time Rottweiler people feel that today's breeders are selecting for a dog that is not sufficiently short-backed nor sufficiently stocky. They feel that too many of today's winning dogs are too rangy, with perhaps a trifle too much "ground covered" (i.e., too long a back). In an effort to interpret standards correctly, it is my opinion that breeders (and judges) should always refer to the *original* standard, too, in their deliberations as to what was being described. With this in mind, the following is a translation of the original German standard.

ORIGINAL GERMAN STANDARD

GENERAL APPEARANCE AND CHARACTER: The Rottweiler is a good-sized, strongly-built, active dog. He is affectionate, intelligent, easily trained to work, naturally obedient, and extremely faithful. While not quarrelsome, he possesses great courage and makes a splendid guard. His demeanor is dignified and he is not excitable.

HEAD: Is of medium length, the skull broad between the ears. Stop well pronounced as is also the occiput. Muzzle is not very long. It should not be longer than the distance from the stop to the occiput. Nose is well developed, with relatively large nostrils and is always black. Flews which should not be too pronounced are also black. Jaws should be strong and muscular; teeth strong—incisors of lower jaw must touch the inner surface of the upper incisors. Eyes are of medium size, dark brown in color and should express faithfulness, good humor, and confidence.

Baldrick vom Hochfeld, also known as "Bear," at nine months (above) and at one year (below). This male was bred by Vivian Peters and is owned by Chris Hagood.

The ears are comparatively small, set high and wide and hang over about on a level with top of head. The skin on head should not be loose. The neck should be of fair length, strong, round and very muscular, slightly arched and free from throatiness.

FOREQUARTERS: Shoulders should be well placed, long and sloping, elbows well let down, but not loose. Legs muscular and with plenty of bone and substance, pasterns straight and strong. Feet strong, round and close, with toes well arched. Soles very hard, toenails dark, short and strong.

BODY: The chest is roomy, broad, and deep. Ribs well sprung. Back straight, strong and rather short. Loins strong and deep, and flanks should not be tucked up. Croup short, broad, but not sloping.

HINDQUARTERS: Upper thigh is short, broad and very muscular. Lower thigh very muscular at top and strong and sinewy at the bottom. Stifles fairly well bent, hocks strong. The hind feet are somewhat longer than the front ones but should be close and strong with toes well arched. There should be no dewclaws.

TAIL: Should be short, placed high (on level with back) and carried horizontally. Dogs are frequently born with a short stump tail, and when tail is too long it must be docked close to body.

COAT: Hair should be short, coarse, and flat. The undercoat which is absolutely required on neck and thighs should not show through outer coat. The hair should be a little longer on the back of front and hind legs and on tail.

COLOR: Black, with clearly defined markings on cheeks, muzzle, chest and legs, as well as over both eyes. Color of markings: tan to mahogany brown. A small spot of white on chest and belly is permissible but not desirable.

200

HEIGHT: Shoulder height for males is 23¾ to 27 inches, for females, 21¾ to 25¾ inches, but height should always be considered in relation to the general appearance and conformation of the dog.

FAULTS: Too lightly built or too heavily built. Sway back. Roach back. Too long body. Lack of spring of ribs. Head too long and narrow, or too short and plump. Lack of occiput, snipy muzzle, cheekiness, topline of muzzle not straight. Light or flesh-colored nose. Hanging flews. Overshot or undershot [jaw]. Loose skin on head. Ears set too low, or ears too heavy. Long or narrow or rose ear, or ears uneven in size. Light, small or slanting eyes, or lack of expression. Neck too long, thin or weak, or very noticeable throatiness. Lack of bone and muscle. Short or straight shoulders. Front legs too close together, or not straight. Weak pasterns. Splay feet, light nails, weak toes. Flat ribs. Sloping croup. Too heavy or plump body. Flanks drawn up. Flat thighs. Cowhocks or weak hocks. Dewclaws. Tail set too high or too low, or one that is too long or too thin. Soft, too short, too long or too open coat. Wavy coat or lack of undercoat. White markings on toes, legs, or other parts of body. Markings not well defined or smudgy. The one-color tan Rottweiler with either black or light mask, or with black streak on back as well as other colors such as brown or blue, are not recognized and are believed to be crossbred, as is also a longhaired Rottweiler. Timid or stupid-appearing animals are to be positively rejected.

Following for comparison is the current American Kennel Club official Rottweiler standard that was adopted in 1981.

MODERN AKC STANDARD

GENERAL APPEARANCE: The ideal Rottweiler is a large, robust and powerful dog, black with clearly defined rust markings. His compact build denotes great strength, agility and endurance. Males are characteristically larger, heavier boned, and more masculine in appearance.

Pomac's Lexa P. Van Lare starts her show career, taking after her sire, Ch. Radio Ranch's Axel v. Notara, and her dam, Ch. Hallmark's "The Sting." Owners: Greg and Lori Benkiser.

SIZE: Males, 24 inches to 27 inches. Females, 22 inches to 25 inches. Proportion should always be considered rather than height alone. The length of the body, from the breastbone (sternum) to the rear edge of the pelvis (ischium) is slightly longer than the height of the dog at the withers; the most desirable proportion being as 10 to 9. Depth of chest should be fifty percent of the height. *Serious faults:* Lack of proportion, undersize, oversize.

HEAD: Of medium length, broad between the ears: forehead line seen in profile is moderately arched. Cheekbones and stop well developed; length of muzzle should not exceed distance between stop and occiput. Skull is preferred dry; however, some wrinkling may occur when dog is alert. *Muzzle:* Bridge is straight, broad at base with slight tapering towards tip. Nose is broad rather than round, with black nostrils. *Lips:* Always black; corners tightly closed. Inner mouth pigment is dark. A pink mouth is to be penalized. *Teeth:* 42 in number (20 upper and 22 lower); strong, correctly placed, meeting in a scissors bite, lower incisors touching inside of upper incisors. *Serious faults:* Any missing teeth, level bite. *Disqualifications:* Undershot, overshot, four or more missing teeth. *Eyes:* Of medium size, moderately deep set, almond-shaped with well-fitting lids. Iris of uniform color, from medium to dark brown, the darker shade always preferred. *Serious faults:* Yellow (bird of prey) eyes; eyes not of same color, eyes unequal in size or shape. Hairless lid. *Ears:* Pendant, proportionately small, triangular in shape; set well apart and placed on skull so as to make it appear broader when the dog is alert. Ear terminates at approximate mid-cheek level. Correctly held, the inner edge will lie tightly against cheek.

NECK: Powerful, well muscled, moderately long with slight arch and without loose skin.

BODY: Topline is firm and level, extending in straight line from withers to croup. *Brisket:* Deep, reaching to elbow. *Chest:* Roomy, broad with well-pronounced forechest. *Ribs:* Well sprung. *Loin:* Short, deep, and well muscled. Croup: Broad, medium length, slightly sloping.

TAIL: Normally carried in horizontal position, giving impression of an elongation of topline. Carried slightly above horizontal when dog is excited. Some dogs are born without a tail, or a very short stub. Tail is normally docked close to the body. The set of the tail is more important than length.

Ch. Der Catlin's H H Dieter, C.D. by Ch. Southwood's H H Blue, C.D. ex Ch. DC's Antje vom Rostock. Bred by Susan C. Catlin of Der Catlin and owned by Vivian Peters of vom Hochfeld.

FOREQUARTERS: Shoulder blade long, well laid back at 45 degree angle. Elbows tight, well under body. Distance from withers to elbow and elbow to ground is equal. *Legs:* Strongly developed with straight heavy bone. Not set closely together. Pasterns: Strong, springy and almost perpendicular to ground. *Feet:* Round, compact, well-arched toes, turning neither in nor out. Pads thick and hard; nails short, strong and black. Dewclaws may be removed.

HINDQUARTERS: Angulation of hindquarters balances that of forequarters. *Upper thigh:* Fairly long, broad and well muscled. *Stifle joint:* Moderately angulated. *Lower thigh:* Long, powerful, extensively muscled leading into a strong hock joint; metatarsus nearly perpendicular to ground. Viewed from rear, hind legs are straight and wide enough apart to fit in with a properly built body. *Feet:* Somewhat longer than front feet, well-arched toes turning neither in nor out. Dewclaws must be removed if present.

204

Am. and Can. Ch. Donnaj Vt Yankee of Paulus, C.D.X., TT going Best of Breed. A working Rottweiler with brains and beauty! Owner: Jan Marshall.

COAT: Outer coat is straight, coarse, dense, medium length, lying flat. Undercoat must be present on neck and thighs, but should not show through the outer coat. The Rottweiler should be exhibited in a natural condition without trimming except to remove whiskers, if desired. *Fault:* Wavy coat. *Serious faults:* Excessively short coat, curly or open coat; lack of undercoat. *Disqualification:* Long coat.

COLOR: Always black with rust to mahogany markings. The borderline between black and rust should be clearly defined. The markings should be located as follows: a spot over each eye; on cheeks, as a strip around each side of the muzzle, but not on the bridge of nose; on throat; triangular mark on either side of breastbone; on forelegs from carpus downward to toes; on inside of rear legs showing down the front of stifle and broadening out to front of rear legs from hock to toes; but not completely eliminating black from back of legs; under tail. Black pencil

Am. and Can. Ch. Rodsden's Kato v. Donnaj, C.D.X., T.D., the first Rottweiler to win Best in Show in the United States. Kato was owner-handled by Jan Marshall to all of his wins.

markings on toes. The undercoat is gray or black. Quantity and location of rust markings is important and should not exceed ten percent of body color. Insufficient or excessive markings should not be penalized: *Serious faults:* Excessive markings; white markings anyplace on dog (a few white hairs do not constitute a marking); light-colored markings. *Disqualifications:* Any base color other than black; total absence of markings.

GAIT: The Rottweiler is a trotter. The motion is harmonious, sure, powerful and unhindered, with a strong fore-reach and a powerful rear drive. Front and rear legs are thrown neither in nor out, as the imprint of hindfeet should touch that of forefeet.

In a trot, the forequarters and hindquarters are mutually coordinated while the back remains firm; as speed is increased legs will converge under body towards a center line.

CHARACTER: The Rottweiler should possess a fearless expression with a self-assured aloofness that does not lend itself to immediate and indiscriminate friendships. He has an inherent desire to protect home and family, and is an intelligent dog of extreme hardness and adaptability with a strong willingness to work. A judge shall dismiss from the ring any shy or vicious Rottweiler. *Shyness:* A dog shall be judged fundamentally shy if, refusing to stand for examination, it shrinks away from the judge; if it fears an approach from the rear; if it shies at sudden or unusual noises to a marked degree. *Viciousness:* A dog that attacks or attempts to attack either the judge or its handler is definitely vicious. An aggressive or belligerent attitude towards other dogs shall not be deemed viciousness.

FAULTS: The foregoing is a description of the ideal Rottweiler. Any structural fault that detracts from the above described working dog must be penalized to the extent of the deviation.

DISQUALIFICATIONS: Undershot, overshot, four or more missing teeth. Long coat. Any base color other than black; total absence of markings.

BRITISH STANDARD

GENERAL APPEARANCE: The Rottweiler is an above-average-sized stalwart dog. His correctly proportioned, compact and powerful form permits of great strength, manoeuverability and endurance. His bearing displays boldness and courage; his tranquil gaze manifests good nature and devotion.

HEAD AND SKULL: The head is of medium length; the skull between the ears is broad. The forehead line is moderately arched as seen from the side. Occipital bone well developed but not conspicuous. Cheeks well muscled but not prominent, with the zygomatic arch well formed. The skin on the head should not be loose although it is allowed to form moderate wrinkle when the dog is attentive. Muzzle fairly deep with topline level and length not longer than the length from stop to occiput.

NOSE: The nose is well developed with proportionately large nostrils and is always black.

EYES: The eyes should be of medium size, almond shaped and dark brown in colour; eyelids close lying.

EARS: The ears are pendant, small in proportion rather than large, set high and wide apart on the head, lying flat and close to the cheek.

MOUTH: The teeth are strong and the incisors of the lower jaw must touch the inner surface of the upper incisors. The flews are black and firm; they fall gradually away towards the corners of the mouth, which do not protrude excessively.

NECK: The neck should be of fair length, strong, round and very muscular. It should be slightly arched and free from throatiness.

FOREQUARTERS: The shoulders should be well placed on the body, long and sloping with the elbows well let down, but not loose. The legs should be muscular with plenty of bone and substance. The pasterns should be bent slightly forward and not be completely vertical. The front legs seen from all sides must be straight and not placed too closely to one another.

BODY: The chest should be roomy, broad and deep with the ribs well sprung. The depth of brisket will not be more, and not much less than 50% of the shoulder height. The back should be straight, strong and not too long; ratio of shoulder height to length of body should be as 9 is to 10; the loins short, strong and

A 1970 photo of Hannibal of Fair Lane, bred by Vivian Peters and owned by Hector and Mary Armenta.

deep, the flanks should not be tucked up. The croup should be broad, of proportionate length, and very slightly sloping.

HINDQUARTERS: The upper thigh not too short, broad and strongly muscled. The lower thigh well muscled at the top and strong and sinewy lower down. Stifles fairly well bent. Hocks well angulated without exaggeration and not completely vertical.

FEET: The feet should be strong, round and compact with the toes well arched. The hind feet are somewhat longer than the front. The pads should be very hard and the toenails short, dark and strong. Rear dewclaws removed.

Ch. Bonnie of Fair Lane, handled by Dave Schneider. Bonnie finished her championship in three months with three "majors" at the age of thirteen months. Breeder/owner: Vivian Peters.

GAIT: In movement the Rottweiler should convey an impression of supple strength, endurance and purpose. While the back remains firm and stable there is a powerful hind thrust and good stride. First and foremost, movement should be harmonious, positive and unrestricted.

TAIL: Carried horizontally. It is short, strong and not set too low. It should be docked at the first joint.

COAT: The coat, which consists of top coat and undercoat, should be of medium length, coarse and flat. The undercoat, which is essential on the neck and thighs, should not show through the outer coat. The hair may also be a little longer on the back of the forelegs and breachings.

COLOUR: The colour is black with clearly defined markings on the cheeks, muzzle, chest and legs, as well as over both eyes and the area beneath the tail. Colour of markings ranges from rich tan to mahogany brown.

SIZE: For males the height at the shoulder should be between 25 and 27 inches and for females between 23 and 25 inches. However, height should always be considered in relation to the general appearance of the dog.

FAULTS: The following faults are noted for the clarification of the Standard.
1. Too lightly or too heavily built.
2. Sway backed or roach backed.
3. Cow hocked, bow hocked, or weak hocked.
4. Long or excessively wavy coat.
5. Any white markings.
6. Nervousness and viciousness are highly undesirable.

NOTE: Male animals should have two apparently normal testicles fully descended into the scrotum.

Ch. Welkerhaus' Rommel, U.D. was the sire of fifteen AKC conformation show champions and is pictured here at age three years. Breeder: Richard H. Werder. Owner: Rita Welker.

Ch. Lucene's Laura, C.D., a bitch owned by breeder/owner Michelle Sudinski, is pictured with Ch. Der Catlin's H H Dieter, C.D. Dieter was bred by Susan C. Catlin and is owned by Vivian Peters.

How could this seven-week-old youngster, Ch. Pomac's Yoda of Dagobah, know that he would become a multi-Best of Breed and Group placer someday? Bred and owned by Patrick and Olga McDonald.

Angus and Atilla vom Hochfeld at seven weeks. Owners: Mike Howard (Angus) and Bud and Shirley Fisher (Atilla). Vivian Peters, breeder.

Going Best of Winners at Birmingham is Ch. Pomac's Troll vom Hihoff, here pictured at eleven months. Sired by Ch. Radio Ranch's Axel v. Notara out of Ch. Hallmark's "The Sting." Breeders: Patrick and Olga McDonald. Owner: Alison Lowe.

Dog Show Glossary

AKC. American Kennel Club.

BAIT. Food tidbits to attract the dog's attention.

BITCH. Female dog.

BREEDER. Owner of a bitch at the time of whelping.

CASTRATED. A male dog with his testicles removed— a show disqualification.

COW-HOCKED. The hock of the leg turn inward.

CROPPED. Ears cut to make them stand erect.

CRYPTORCHID. Male dog with no descended testicles—a show disqualification.

DAM. Female with puppies, mother.

DEW CLAW. Extra toe on the inside of the hind legs.

DOCKED. Tail cut to a certain length.

DOG. Male dog.

FEATHERING. Long, often downy hair on legs, ears, and tail.

GAIT. To move the dog around the ring, movement.

HACKLES. Hair on the back of the neck.

HEAT. Estrus, the seasonal period of the bitch.

HIP DYSPLASIA. A genetic hip disorder.

INBREEDING. Mating closely-related dogs.

Ch. Der Catlin's H H Dieter, C.D. (above and below) bred by Susan Catlin and owned by Vivian Peters.

Jenek's Mandy, owned by Vivian Peters, portrays that intelligent look of our breed (above) but strikes a more serious pose (below).

Ch. Inner Sanctums Oh Jezebel, C.D. and Ch. Pomac's Graf Tanzer, owned by Greg and Lori Benkiser, are the best of friends (above and below). Both were sired by Am. and Can. Ch. Graudstark's Pegasus, C.D. "Jez" was out of Inner Sanctums Phoebe and "Tan" was out of Ch. Hallmark's "The Sting."

LEVEL BITE. The upper and lower front teeth meet edge to edge.

LITTER. The puppies from one whelping.

MAJOR. A win of three or more points in show competition.

MONORCHID. Male dog with only one descended testicle—a show disqualification.

OUTCROSS. Mating dogs with no common ancestors within five generations.

OVERSHOT. The upper front teeth project beyond the lower teeth.

PASTERN. The leg below the knee.

PEDIGREE. A written history of a dog's ancestors (usually three or more generations).

PRICKED. Ears that stand erect naturally.

RUFF. The thick hair around the neck.

SCISSORS BITE. The inside of the upper front teeth meet the outside of the lower teeth.

SIRE. The male parent of a litter.

SOUNDNESS. Whether or not a dog is in good physical and mental condition.

SPAYED. A female whose ovaries have been surgically removed—a show disqualification.

SPECIAL. A champion.

STACK. To position the dog for examination by the judge.

STIFLE. Knee.

STUD. Male dog used for breeding purposes.

THROATY. Too much skin around the neck.

UNDERSHOT. The lower front teeth project above the upper teeth.

WHELPING. The birth of a litter of puppies.

WITHERS. The highest point of the shoulders.

Index